THE ENRON CORPORATION:
Corporate Complicity in Human Rights Violations

Human Rights Watch
New York · Washington · London · Brussels

Copyright © January 1999 by Human Rights Watch
All rights reserved.
Printed in the United States of America.

ISBN 1-56432-197-5
Library of Congress Catalog Card Number: 98-83147
Cover photo: Arvind Ganesan

Addresses for Human Rights Watch
350 Fifth Avenue, 34th Floor, New York, NY 10118-3299
Tel: (212) 290-4700, Fax: (212) 736-1300, E-mail: hrwnyc@hrw.org

1522 K Street, N.W., #910, Washington, DC 20005-1202
Tel: (202) 371-6592, Fax: (202) 371-0124, E-mail: hrwdc@hrw.org

33 Islington High Street, N1 9LH London, UK
Tel: (171) 713-1995, Fax: (171) 713-1800, E-mail: hrwatchuk@gn.apc.org

15 Rue Van Campenhout, 1000 Brussels, Belgium
Tel: (2) 732-2009, Fax: (2) 732-0471, E-mail: hrwatcheu@gn.apc.org

Web Site Address: http://www.hrw.org

Listserv address: To subscribe to the list, send an e-mail message to majordomo@igc.apc.org with "subscribe hrw-news" in the body of the message (leave the subject line blank).

Human Rights Watch is dedicated to
protecting the human rights of people around the world.

We stand with victims and activists to prevent
discrimination, to uphold political freedom, to protect people from inhumane
conduct in wartime, and to bring offenders to justice.

We investigate and expose
human rights violations and hold abusers accountable.

We challenge governments and those who hold power to end abusive practices
and respect international human rights law.

We enlist the public and the international
community to support the cause of human rights for all.

HUMAN RIGHTS WATCH

Human Rights Watch conducts regular, systematic investigations of human rights abuses in some seventy countries around the world. Our reputation for timely, reliable disclosures has made us an essential source of information for those concerned with human rights. We address the human rights practices of governments of all political stripes, of all geopolitical alignments, and of all ethnic and religious persuasions. Human Rights Watch defends freedom of thought and expression, due process and equal protection of the law, and a vigorous civil society; we document and denounce murders, disappearances, torture, arbitrary imprisonment, discrimination, and other abuses of internationally recognized human rights. Our goal is to hold governments accountable if they transgress the rights of their people.

Human Rights Watch began in 1978 with the founding of its Europe and Central Asia division (then known as Helsinki Watch). Today, it also includes divisions covering Africa, the Americas, Asia, and the Middle East. In addition, it includes three thematic divisions on arms, children's rights, and women's rights. It maintains offices in New York, Washington, Los Angeles, London, Brussels, Moscow, Dushanbe, Rio de Janeiro, and Hong Kong. Human Rights Watch is an independent, nongovernmental organization, supported by contributions from private individuals and foundations worldwide. It accepts no government funds, directly or indirectly.

The staff includes Kenneth Roth, executive director; Michele Alexander, development director; Reed Brody, advocacy director; Carroll Bogert, communications director; Cynthia Brown, program director; Barbara Guglielmo, finance and administration director; Jeri Laber special advisor; Lotte Leicht, Brussels office director; Patrick Minges, publications director; Susan Osnos, associate director; Jemera Rone, counsel; Wilder Tayler, general counsel; and Joanna Weschler, United Nations representative. Jonathan Fanton is the chair of the board. Robert L. Bernstein is the founding chair.

The regional directors of Human Rights Watch are Peter Takirambudde, Africa; José Miguel Vivanco, Americas; Sidney Jones, Asia; Holly Cartner, Europe and Central Asia; and Hanny Megally, Middle East and North Africa. The thematic division directors are Joost R. Hiltermann, arms; Lois Whitman, children's; and Regan Ralph, women's.

The members of the board of directors are Jonathan Fanton, chair; Lisa Anderson, Robert L. Bernstein, William Carmichael, Dorothy Cullman, Gina Despres, Irene Diamond, Adrian W. DeWind, Fiona Druckenmiller, Edith Everett, James C. Goodale, Vartan Gregorian, Alice H. Henkin, Stephen L. Kass, Marina Pinto Kaufman, Bruce Klatsky, Harold Hongju Koh, Alexander MacGregor, Josh Mailman, Samuel K. Murumba, Andrew Nathan, Jane Olson, Peter Osnos, Kathleen Peratis, Bruce Rabb, Sigrid Rausing, Anita Roddick, Orville Schell, Sid Sheinberg, Gary G. Sick, Malcolm Smith, Domna Stanton, and Maya Wiley. Robert L. Bernstein is the founding chair of Human Rights Watch.

TABLE OF CONTENTS

I. Summary and Recommendations 1
    Recommendations 5
        To the Government of India 5
        To the Enron Corporation 5
        To the Government of the United States 8
        To Private and Public Financial Institutions that Financed the Dabhol
            Power Project 8

II. Background: New Delhi and Bombay 10
    Political Opposition to the Project 25
    The Munde Committee Report 26
    The "Renegotiated" Project 29
    The CITU Lawsuit 31

III. Background to the Protests: Ratnagiri District 38
    Land Acquisition 42
    Environmental Degradation 44
        Fresh water 45
        Contamination of salt water 47
    Warnings of Protests 48
    Organization of Opposition to the Project 50

IV. Legal Restrictions Used to Suppress Opposition to the Dabhol Power
    Project 52
    The Bombay Police Act 53
    The Code of Criminal Procedure 55
    The Indian Penal Code 56

V. Ratnagiri: Violations of Human Rights 1997 58
    Arrests of Protesters 59
    Targeting of Protest Leaders 65
        Medha Patkar and B.G. Kolse-Patil: March 1997 66
        Medha Patkar: May 1997 67
        Externment orders: 1996-97 74
        Arrests at Guhagar police station: January 1997 75
        Sadanand Pawar: February 1997 77
    Abuse of the Indian Penal Code 78
        Regarding property damage 79
        Regarding disputes with DPC contractors and police 81
            Katalwadi Village: April 1997 87
            Sanjay Pawar: February 1997 92
            Veldur raid: June 1997 95

VI. The Applicable Laws 100
    International Law 100
    The Laws of India 102

VII. Complicity: The Dabhol Power Corporation 104

VIII. Responsibility: Financing Institutions and the Government of the
    United States 112
    Phase I Financing 113
    The U.S. Government 115
    Phase II Financing 122

IX. Conclusion 125

Appendix A: Correspondence Between Human Rights Watch and the Export-Import
    Bank of the United States 128

Appendix B: Report of the Cabinet Sub-Committee to Review the Dabhol
    Power Project 133

Appendix C: Selected Recommendations and Conclusions from the Parliamentary
    Standing Committee on Energy, May 29, 1995 155

Appendix D: Correspondence Between the Government of India and the
    World Bank 158

Key Individuals Named in this Report

Montek Singh Ahluwalia: Former secretary of the Indian government's Department of Economic Affairs at the Ministry of Finance.
M.I. Beg: Chairman and ex-officio secretary of the Indian government's Central Electricity Authority.
Mangesh Chavan: A local activist in Ratnagiri.
V. Deshmukh: A circle inspector in Ratnagiri district.
Bobby Farris: General manager of the Enron Power Development Corporation.
Y.P. Gambhir: Chairman of the Indian government's Central Electricity Authority.
Joëlle Chassard: Senior financial analyst of the World Bank Energy Operations Division, India Country Department.
B.G. Kolse-Patil: Former Bombay High Court Justice and leader of protests against the Dabhol Power project.
Manohar Joshi: Current chief minister of the state of Maharashtra under the Shiv Sena-BJP government.
Sanjeev Khandekar: Vice President for Community Relations for the Dabhol Power Corporation.
S.D. Khare: Former secretary of the Rashtriya Swayamsewak Sangh (RSS). Residing in the village of Guhagar, Khare is a local leader of opposition to the Dabhol Power project and provides legal aid to villagers arrested for their participation in protests against the project.
Rebecca Mark: Formerly chief executive officer of the Enron Power Development Corporation. Currently the chief executive officer of Azurix, Enron's water development corporation.
Vivek Monteiro: Secretary general of the Center of Indian Trade Unions.
U.K. Mukhopadhyay: Maharashtra government's secretary of energy.
Gopinath Munde: Current deputy chief minister of Maharashtra.
Ajit Nimbalkar: Chairman of the Maharashtra State Electricity Board.
Hazel O'Leary: Former secretary of Energy of the government of the United States.
Medha Patkar: An internationally and nationally recognized environmental activist. Chairperson of the National Alliance for People's Movements (NAPM), a national environmental organization which led demonstrations against the Dabhol Power project.
Sadanand Pawar: A professor of economics in Bombay. Originally from Pawarsakari village near the Dabhol Power project. A recognized leader of local protests against the company.

Sharad Pawar: Former Chief Minister of Maharashtra
N. Raghunathan: Chief secretary of the Maharashtra government's Department of Industries, Energy and Labour.
N. Ramji: Joint secretary of the Indian government's Ministry of Power.
M.S. Rane: Bombay High Court Justice who sat on the two-judge division bench which heard *Center of Indian Trade Unions and others v. Union of India and others*.
V.V.R.K. Rao: Secretary of the Indian government's Central Electricity Authority.
P.G. Satoshe: Assistant sub-inspector at the Guhagar police station.
Howard Schweitzer: Counsel for administration in the office of the general counsel of the Export-Import Bank of the United States.
Sunip Sen: Bombay High Court lawyer who represented the plaintiffs in the *Center of Indian Trade Unions and others v. Union of India and others*.
B.P. Seraf: Bombay High Court Justice who sat on the two-judge division bench which heard *Center of Indian Trade Unions and others v. Union of India and others*.
M.B. Shah: Chief justice of the Bombay High Court.
B.N. Srikrishna: Bombay High Court Justice who initially heard the case *Center for Indian Trade Unions and others v. Union of India and others*.
Joseph Sutton: Chief operating officer for the Enron Corporation. Formerly the managing director of the Dabhol Power Corporation.
A.N. Varma: Chairman of the Indian government's Foreign Investment Promotion Board.
R. Vasudevan: Secretary of the Indian government's Ministry of Power.
Seth Vedantham: Chief engineer of the Indian government's Central Electricity Authority.
Heinz Vergin: World Bank's India country department director.
Frank Wisner: Former United States Ambassador to India.

I. Summary and Recommendations

Human Rights Watch's mission is to protect and advance human rights, and our research and advocacy on corporate responsibility is shaped by these concerns alone. Human Rights Watch takes no position on trade or development policies *per se*. But in an interconnected world where very large and influential transnational corporations compete for finite resources and new markets, human rights and trade are increasingly intertwined. Companies that trade in essential commodities—oil, gas, or electricity—exemplify this phenomenon. In recent years, the energy industry has been embroiled in controversy because of its alleged involvement in situations of human rights violations throughout the world. Some high-profile examples are Royal Dutch/Shell's operations in Nigeria; British Petroleum's development of the Cusiana-Cupiagua oil fields in Colombia; and alleged human rights violations that occurred during Total and Unocal's construction of the Yadana gas pipeline in Burma and Thailand.

Another energy company that warrants attention is the Enron Power Development Corporation, a subsidiary of the Houston-based Enron Corporation, which is one of the world's largest energy companies. Traditionally viewed as a natural gas and oil company, it began to develop electricity projects as an outlet for its natural gas in the early 1990s. In 1997, its annual revenues were more than U.S. $20 billion.

This report focuses on a subsidiary of the Enron Development Corporation in India: the Dabhol Power Corporation (DPC). The DPC's project in the state of Maharashtra constitutes the largest single foreign investment in India, and its history, since 1992, raises questions intrinsic to any serious discussion of the importance of human rights concerns to governments and companies designing investment strategies.

The report details the development of the Dabhol Power project from its inception in 1992 through 1998 in order to illustrate and unbroken continuum: the immense influence that Enron exercised over the central and Maharashtra governments; to describe the company's interaction with villagers—whose legitimate concerns for their livelihood and environment were ignored or dismissed—leading them eventually to oppose the project; to make clear that various avenues to address their concerns about the project—judicial proceedings and direct dialogue with the company—had been exhausted in ways that raised questions rather than answering them. The local opposition that formed to protest the project's lack of transparency, its human impact, its threat to villagers' livelihoods, and its potential to do environmental damage was the affected population's last recourse. Except in one case of stone-throwing and another incident where a water pipeline was broken, the opposition did not resort to violence; villagers' groups did not endorse sabotage, and their methods were peaceful. Yet they were met with serious, sometimes brutal human rights violations carried out on behalf of the state's and the company's interests. The relationship between the controversies surrounding implementation of the project, the efforts to challenge its development, and violations of human rights are all described in detail here because each is an integral part of a complex, disturbing situation.

In 1992, as part of an effort to liberalize the economy, the government of India announced that it was privatizing its energy sector. In the middle of 1992, the government of Maharashtra state announced that the Enron Corporation would build the largest electricity generating plant in the world for Maharashtra at a cost of approximately $3 billion. The operating company would be known as the Dabhol Power Corporation—a joint venture of three U.S. companies: the Enron Corporation, General Electric, and the Bechtel Corporation. Enron is the overseer of the company, originally holding 80 percent ownership. General Electric and Bechtel each hold 10 percent. In November 1998, the Maharashtra government's Maharashtra State Electricity Board (MSEB) bought a 30 percent share of the DPC from Enron, reducing Enron's stake to 50 percent.

The agreement was fast-tracked, running counter to the reservations of key Indian and international economists and condemned by intellectuals, academics, the Indian press, trade unions, opposition political parties, and nongovernmental organizations throughout India. Criticized for lack of transparency, its projected high costs, and potential environmental impacts, the deal was so controversial that when the Shiv Sena-BJP government coalition was elected to power in 1995, it suspended the project. Then, in an about-face that renewed allegations of corruption surrounding the project, the Shiv Sena-BJP government renegotiated the project and allowed its construction. While the project was the focus of attention nationally and internationally because of the controversies surrounding the project's suspension, less attention was given to a pattern of serious human rights violations that the project provoked in localities near the project site, in Maharashtra state.

Leading Indian environmental activists and representatives of villagers' organizations in the affected area organized to oppose the project and, as a direct result of their opposition, have been subjected to beatings and repeated short-term detention. In many cases, they have been detained for periods ranging from several days to two weeks without being produced before a magistrate as required under Indian law. During mass arrests at demonstrations in villages surrounding the project site, protesters have been beaten with canes (*lathis*) or otherwise assaulted by the police, in some cases sustaining severe injuries. Police have also tear-gassed peaceful demonstrations. Police have frequently used laws providing for preventative detention to arrest demonstrators in anticipation of protests, sometimes under suspicion of violence.

Governments have authority to counter any genuine threat to public order; in the case of protests against the Dabhol Power Corporation, some of the charges brought against activists opposed to the company include alleged acts of spontaneous violence—stone-throwing by protesters on one occasion and damage to a water pipeline on another. However, examining the state's response to opposition to the Dabhol Power Corporation, Human Rights Watch believes that the state government of Maharashtra has engaged in a systematic pattern of suppression of freedom of expression and peaceful assembly coupled with arbitrary detentions, excessive use of force, and threats. In the thirty demonstrations directly researched by Human Rights Watch, and in others studied by Indian human rights monitors, there occurred only two minor, unplanned incidents bordering on violence; the character of the opposition protests were peaceful. The police have also misused preventative detention laws to detain people for the peaceful expression of their views. The state has also tolerated the failure of the police to investigate or prosecute perpetrators of attacks on opponents of the Dabhol Power project. The arrests violate the internationally recognized rights of freedom of expression, assembly, movement, protection against unjust arrest and detention, and they constitute police mistreatment. The failure to investigate or prosecute those who have attacked demonstrators represents negligent and biased behavior by police.

In addition to the state, Human Rights Watch believes that the Dabhol Power Corporation and its parent company Enron are complicit in these human rights violations. Enron's local entity, the Dabhol Power Corporation, benefited directly from an official policy of suppressing dissent through misuse of the law, harassment of anti-Enron protest leaders and prominent environmental activists, and police practices ranging from arbitrary to brutal. The company did not speak out about human rights violations and, when questioned about them, chose to dismiss them altogether.

But the Dabhol Power Corporation's responsibility, and by extension that of the consortium and principally Enron, goes beyond a failure to speak out about human rights violations by the state police. The company, under provisions of law, paid the abusive state forces for the security they provided to the company. These forces, located adjacent to the project site, were only stationed there to deal with protests. In addition, contractors (for DPC) engaged in a pattern of harassment, intimidation, and attacks on individuals opposed to the Dabhol Power project. When the victims of these acts attempted to file complaints with the police, they were met with official silence. Police refused to investigate complaints, and in several cases, arrested the victims for acts they did not commit. When these activities were brought to the company's attention, the Dabhol Power Corporation refused to acknowledge that its contractors were responsible for criminal acts and did not adequately investigate, condemn, or cease relationships with these individuals.

Other institutions bear responsibility for human rights violations as well. Human Rights Watch considers that the financiers of Phase I of the project's construction (1992-99) and U.S. government agencies that financed and lobbied for the project are complicit in the human rights violations. In particular, the U.S. government bears special responsibility because of its aggressive lobbying on behalf of the three U.S.-based companies developing the project and because it extended hundreds of millions of dollars in public funds for the project while seemingly indifferent human rights-related conditionalities that apply to such transactions.

Human Rights Watch also considers that those institutions which have agreed to finance Phase II (set to begin in 1999) will be complicit in human rights violations unless they implement adequate safeguards to ensure respect for human rights. Legal prohibitions on peaceful freedom of expression and assembly are still in force in the districts near the DPC site; many of the cases against activists are still pending, affecting the daily lives, income, and future liberty of the individuals involved; and the company receiving funding has made no attempt to correct the practices that violate human rights.

Human Rights Watch calls on the actors involved in this project—the government of Maharashtra, the government of India, the Enron Corporation, the government of the United States, and public and private financial institutions—to take concrete measures to investigate and punish the perpetrators of these violations; to take specific measures to ensure that human rights protections are integrated into project development; and to prevent further abuses.

This report is based on a six-week investigation in India during January and February 1998 and follow-up investigations in Washington, D.C. and New York. Human Rights Watch interviewed dozens of witnesses and victims of human rights violations; Indian government officials; lawyers knowledgeable about the events; current and former U.S. government officials; and representatives of nongovernmental organizations. Press reports, legal documents, reports by local human rights organizations, and more than 1,200 pages of internal company and government documents were reviewed for the investigation. Appended to the report are the correspondence between Human Rights Watch and the Export-Import Bank of the United States, the Maharashtra government's *Report of the*

Summary and Recommendations 5

Cabinet Sub-Committee to Review the Dabhol Power Project, selected conclusions and recommendations from the Indian government's Parliamentary Standing Committee on Energy, and correspondence between the government of India and the World Bank concerning the economic viability of the Dabhol Power project.

Recommendations

To the Government of India

- Respect the rights of all individuals, including those in communities near the Dabhol Power project, to exercise freedom of expression, association and peaceful assembly and cease harassment of activists opposed to the Dabhol Power project in its current form.

- Allow members of nongovernmental organizations formed to challenge the operations of the transnational corporations to meet and campaign.

- Ensure that the police response to demonstrations and opposition to the Dabhol Power project is in full compliance with international standards.

- Appoint an independent judicial inquiry to determine how the Bombay Police Act, the Code of Criminal Procedure, and the Indian Penal Code have been abused in order to suppress freedom of expression and peaceful assembly and to formulate recommendations to ensure that such abuse is prevented.

- Appoint an independent judicial inquiry into the actions of the security forces in Ratnagiri district, make public the findings of the inquiry, bring to trial those found to be responsible for human rights abuses, and ensure that the rights of individuals opposed to the Dabhol Power project are respected.

- In the context of the human rights crisis that occurred during the construction of Phase I of the Dabhol Power project, appoint an independent oversight body to review the situation of human rights related to Phase I of the Dabhol Power project in order to ensure that past human rights violations are remedied and to formulate guidelines so that further abuses do not take place during the construction of Phase II of the project.

To the Enron Corporation

- Urge the Maharashtra government not to obstruct the exercise of peaceful freedom of assembly and freedom of association and expression, particularly with respect to grievances directed against the Dabhol Power Corporation. In particular, publicly and privately call on the Maharashtra government to lift Section 37 of the Bombay Police Act in districts surrounding the project.

- Publicly and privately condemn human rights abuses by Maharashtra police in the area where the company is operating, both in general and in specific cases, and make clear that activities undertaken related to the Dabhol Power project must be in accordance with international human rights standards.

- Encourage the Maharashtra and central governments to appoint an independent public inquiry into the actions of the security forces in the areas impacted by the Dabhol Power project and to bring to trial those found to be responsible for abuses.

- Make public all details relating to security arrangements for the protection of the Dabhol Power Corporation's facilities, including private security contracts and any arrangements with government security forces, including legal and private arrangements between the state and the Dabhol Power Corporation.

- Conduct a credible investigation to determine the role of the company and its personnel in human rights violations that occurred during construction of Phase I of the Dabhol Power project.

- Investigate allegations that contractors to the Dabhol Power Corporation threatened, harassed, and attacked individuals opposed to the Dabhol Power project. Make public all findings of such an investigation. In cases where contractors committed these acts, terminate the company's relationship with these contractors.

- Refrain from funding or sponsoring nongovernmental organizations (NGOs) without proper community consultation in order to ensure that such sponsorship does not have a destabilizing effect on local communities and does not lead to violence.

- Review programs of community assistance to ensure that development projects are planned by people who are professionally trained, that communities are genuinely engaged on a participatory basis in development plans, and that projects address the actual needs of the people in those communities. Consider establishing independent, professionally administered bodies for the implementation of development projects.

- Adopt explicit company policies stating an unqualified respect for human rights and establish procedures to ensure that company activities do not result in human rights abuses. Such procedures should involve monitoring by company, governmental, and nongovernmental actors and should be fully transparent.

- Appoint high-ranking corporate officials to monitor human rights in the project area and to denounce the use of unjustified or excessive force. These officials should have a knowledge of international, national, and state-level human rights standards and current best practices by corporations to respect human rights.

- Given the financial relationship between the company and abusive police forces, the company should conduct a full review to identify police officers who committed human rights violations. When evidence of human rights violations is found, the company should terminate its relationship with such officers.

- Produce annual reports to shareholders on the company's activities in Ratnagiri, including information on the nature and extent of the company's relations with the Maharashtra government and measures taken to prevent human rights abuses by the state police.

- Allow independent verification, by national and/or international NGOs, of compliance by the company with international, national, and state-level human rights and environmental standards.

- When new facilities or investments are planned, carry out a "human rights impact assessment," identifying in particular problems related to security provision and conflict resolution, in addition to the legally required "environmental impact assessment," and develop plans to avoid the problems identified by such assessments.

To the Government of the United States
- Publicly condemn all human rights violations that occurred as a result of the Dabhol Power project and urge the Indian government to investigate allegations of human rights violations.

- Make public the human rights impact assessment conducted by the Export-Import Bank of the United States on the Dabhol Power project under the human rights policy of the Export-Import Bank.

- Verify and make public whether the Export-Import Bank of the United States considered information about human rights before extending financing to the Dabhol Power project, as required under Section 2(b)(1)(B) of the Export-Import Bank Act of 1945.

- Verify and make public whether the Department of State conducted a study of human rights and provided this information to the Export-Import Bank, as required under Export-Import Bank policy.

- Amend legislation governing transactions by the Export-Import Bank of the United States to ensure that human rights violations are a condition for suspension of U.S. government assistance to transnational corporations.

- Conduct an audit, through the General Accounting Office or other government agencies, of all public funds used to finance the Dabhol Power project.

To Private and Public Financial Institutions that Financed the Dabhol Power Project
- For public and private institutions that financed the Dabhol Power project, adopt explicit policies in support of human rights and establish procedures to ensure that financing of projects does not contribute to or result in human rights abuses. At a minimum, implement a policy to conduct a "human rights impact assessment." Such procedures should involve governmental and nongovernmental actors and should be fully transparent.

- Require that high-ranking officials within financing institutions be appointed to monitor human rights in relation to the Dabhol Power project financing and subsequent human rights developments as Phase I is completed and Phase II begins.

- In order to verify compliance of human rights standards, private institutions who are financing the Dabhol Power project should produce annual reports to shareholders on the company's activities in terms of human rights. Public institutions that are financing the project should report to the public annually in order to demonstrate compliance with these policies.

II. Background: New Delhi and Bombay

In 1992, pursuing a policy of economic liberalization, the Congress (I)-led government of India, under then Prime Minister P.V. Narasimha Rao, announced that it would open up the power and electricity sector to foreign investment. On a three-week trip abroad, during May and June 1992, a senior Indian government delegation met with Enron officials and announced that the company was interested in building a power plant in India.[1]

On June 10, 1992, almost immediately after the delegation's trip, the Indian government's secretary of power informed the Maharashtra State Electricity Board (MSEB) that a group of Enron officials was coming to survey land along the coast of Maharashtra for a proposed power project. Five days later, representatives of Enron and General Electric arrived in New Delhi and met with officials of the central government about the proposed project. Two days after that, the company delegation arrived in Bombay and reviewed sites along the coast.[2] Following their survey, they met with representatives of the government of Maharashtra, and on June 20, 1992, a Memorandum of Understanding (MoU) with the state government was signed to build the Dabhol Power project. The operating entity would be known as the Dabhol Power Corporation (DPC), a joint venture of Enron, General Electric, and the Bechtel Corporation.[3] In the eyes of the public, the DPC was Enron, and it is often colloquially referred to as "the Enron project," "Enron," or "the Enron Power project."

Although the MoU was not a legally binding document, the deal-making process was criticized for its haste, its lack of transparency, and the absence of competitive bidding. The process would form the basis for a widespread belief that corruption played a role in the project's implementation. Detailed criticism of the

---

[1] The Munde Committee, *Report of the Cabinet Sub-Committee to Review the Dabhol Power Project*, Bombay, August 1995, pp. 8-12. Background on the committee and its report is provided below in this section. Report on file at Human Rights Watch.

[2] Ibid.

[3] Memorandum of Understanding between the Maharashtra State Electricity Board, the Enron Power Corporation, and the General Electric Corporation, June 20, 1992. Memorandum of Understanding on file at Human Rights Watch. The Dabhol Power Corporation is a consortium in which Enron is an 80 percent shareholder and General Electric and Bechtel each hold 10 percent of the shares. On November 3, 1998, the ownership structure changed when the Maharashtra State Electricity Board (MSEB) purchased a 30 percent stake of Enron's 80 percent share of the DPC for approximately $151 million at the November 1998 rupee-dollar exchange rate.

agreement was provided in the Maharashtra government's 1995 *Report of the Cabinet Sub-Committee to Review the Dabhol Power Project*, which stated:

> Thus, in a matter of less than three days after its [the delegation's] arrival in Bombay, an MoU was signed between Enron and MSEB in a matter involving a project of the value of over Rs. 10,000 crores [almost $3 billion] at the time, with entirely imported fuel and largely imported equipment, in which, admittedly, no one in the Government had expertise or experience. In fact, the file [on the project] does not even show what Enron was—what its history is, business or accomplishment. It looked more like an ad hoc decision rather than a considered decision on a durable arrangement with a party after obtaining adequate and reliable information. Neither the balance sheet and annual accounts of Enron, nor any information about its activities, area of operation, its associates, etc. was obtained by the government then, or even later.[4]

After the agreement was signed, the government of Maharashtra state requested that the World Bank review the project in order to determine what would be required by the companies and the government and to evaluate the MoU.

The World Bank team found many irregularities in the agreement and noted that the government had not set up an overarching framework within which to privatize power in India. The World Bank's analysis determined that the government had not provided an "overall economic justification of this project" and, in particular, noted that the MoU required the MSEB to pay the company within sixty days, but the company had no limitations on actual supply of electricity, importing fuel, construction, or financing. In other words, the MSEB would have to pay the company for electricity at a prescribed rate, regardless of whether the electricity was actually available. The World Bank thus determined that the MoU was "one-sided" in favor of Enron and encouraged the government to "verify Enron's experience" as an electricity generating company before proceeding with the project.[5]

The World Bank's doubts were echoed by the government of India's Central Electricity Authority (CEA), whose experts conducted their own analysis of the MoU and also noted many irregularities in the agreement. Among their findings,

---

[4] *Report of the Cabinet Sub-Committee...*, p. 12.

[5] Letter from Joëile Chassard, World Bank senior financial analyst, Energy Operations Division, India Country Department to U.K. Mukhophadhyay, Maharashtra state secretary for energy and environment, July 8, 1992. Letter on file at Human Rights Watch.

they reported that the MoU did not provide specific details about the costs of the project which were required under Indian law; that the MoU did not specify when the twenty-year contract (and its associated payments) would begin, when the electricity was available, or when the contract was signed; the structure of payments was a "departure from existing norms"; the price of power was high; there was no provision to audit the project over time to ensure that the price MSEB paid to the company was commensurate to the actual cost of electricity; the MSEB had agreed to a guaranteed minimum fuel purchase, while the fuel supplier was not concurrently bound to provide a minimum quantity of fuel; and the MSEB had not verified whether the price of fuel was economical. Consequently, the CEA concluded that the "entire MoU is one sided" in favor of Enron and its partners.[6]

On August 29, 1992, Enron submitted its detailed application to the Indian government's Foreign Investment Promotion Board for a $3.1 billion project to generate 2,550 megawatts of electricity fueled by liquefied natural gas (LNG). The plan envisaged that the power plant would go on-line in December 1995.[7]

Shortly thereafter, on September 9, 1992, Linklaters & Paines, a United Kingdom-based law firm hired by Enron, submitted a report to the Indian government titled "Problems Concerning the Application of the Indian Electricity Acts." The report was commissioned to highlight discrepancies within the Electricity (Supply) Act, 1948, which regulated state-owned electricity generating enterprises, and the proposed private sector power project. Based on their analysis, Linklaters & Paines made several recommendations to accommodate the project, including:

> amending legislation (although we [Linklaters & Paines] understand that this is regarded prima facie as politically impracticable);
> further administrative direction or notification, or, to modify the tariff structure published under section 43-A;

---

[6] "CEA's Comments on the Proposed MoU," enclosed with a letter from M.I. Beg, chairman and ex-officio secretary, Central Electricity Authority to R. Vasudevan, secretary, Ministry of Power, August 7, 1992. Letter on file at Human Rights Watch.

[7] Letter from Rebecca Mark, president and chief executive officer, Enron Power Development Corporation to A.N. Varma, chairman, Foreign Investment Promotion Board, August 28, 1992. Letter on file at Human Rights Watch. According to the letter, the total cost of the project was estimated at $3.1 billion: $2.1 billion for the power plant, $845 million for related Liquefied Natural Gas (LNG) facilities, and the remaining $155 million in unspecified expenses.

contractual undertakings from GOI [Government of India] and/or MSEB regarding the practical application of the relevant provisions in the case of the Dabhol Power Project; and the issue of legal opinions for the benefit of sponsors and letters by GOI's and MSEB advisers.[8]

In other words, the company's lawyers were requesting that the government modify the law particularly in regard to accounting procedures, purchasing agreements, and judicial and public scrutiny to facilitate the project. Later, the Maharashtra State Electricity Board wrote a letter to the government noting that private companies, and DPC in particular, would not want to be subject to public or judicial review, in particular, scrutiny flowing from statutory provisions requiring the company to operate efficiently. That letter states:

> Thus, DPC even though [it] may be a private sector company under the Companies Act, 1956 will have cast upon it statutory duties and to the extent is likely to be subject in the due performance of such duties to public and judicial scrutiny. This may not be acceptable to foreign promoters. One such area of scrutiny would be the duty cast... "to operate and maintain in the most efficient and economical matter the generating stations."[9]

The MSEB thus proposed that standards under various Indian laws should be modified to attract foreign investors, including provisions that would make private projects more transparent.

Through the rest of the year, more clarifications and opinions were sought about the project within various government agencies. Then, on December 12, 1992, the Foreign Investment Promotion Board notified Enron that its project would have to be scaled down to 1,920 megawatts (from 2,550) and split into two phases. The price would be $2.65 billion as opposed to the original $3.1 billion.

---

[8] Linklaters & Paines, "Dabhol Power Project: Problems Concerning the Application of the Indian Electricity Acts," September 4, 1992, p. 6. Memorandum on file at Human Rights Watch.

[9] Memorandum from Ajit Nimbalkar, chairman, Maharashtra State Electricity Board, to N. Ramji, joint secretary, Ministry of Power, September 21, 1992. Memorandum on file at Human Rights Watch.

The company agreed to the revised project.[10]   On February 3, 1993, the government of India notified Enron that its project had been approved and that the government would apply for financing with the World Bank and other institutions.[11]

The World Bank turned down financing for the project on April 30, 1993. It determined that the project was "not economically viable."[12] Later, the state of Maharashtra empowered a Cabinet sub-committee, known as the Munde Committee, to review the project. The committee analyzed the series of events leading up to the World Bank's decision and reported:

> [I]t is difficult to appreciate when and why the decision to split the project...was taken. Nor is it clear that this was done after careful consideration of the requirements of the MSEB and the State of Maharashtra. In fact, it seems to address only the concerns of Enron. The conduct of the negotiations shows that the sole objective was to see that Enron was not displeased—it is as if Enron was doing a favour by this deal to India and to Maharashtra. In fact, the entire negotiation with Enron is an illustration of how not to negotiate, how not to take a weak position in negotiations and how not to leave the initiative to the other side.[13]

The project continued to move forward, nevertheless. Enron, in a letter to the MSEB, said that it would change the World Bank's opinion and secure financing from the bank.[14] Upon an application by the MSEB to reconsider its decision, the World Bank reaffirmed its refusal to finance the project and criticized the MSEB for claiming that, without the project, MSEB's future ability to efficiently provide

---

[10] Office of the Prime Minister, government of India, "Summary Record of the Foreign Investment Promotion Board (FIPB) Meeting Held on 5th December, 1992," December 9, 1992. Record on file at Human Rights Watch.

[11] Letter from the government of India, Ministry of Industry, Department of Industrial Development, Secretariat for Industrial Approvals, to the Enron Power Development Corporation, February 3, 1993. Letter on file at Human Rights Watch.

[12] Letter from Heinz Vergin, India country department director, the World Bank, to Montek Singh Ahluwalia, secretary, Department of Economic Affairs, Ministry of Finance of the government of India, April 30, 1993. Letter on file at Human Rights Watch.

[13] *Report of the Cabinet Sub-Committee...*, p. 18.

[14] Letter from Joseph Sutton, chief operating officer of Enron, to Ajit Nimbalkar, chairman, Maharashtra State Electricity Board, June 23, 1993. Letter on file at Human Rights Watch.

electricity to consumers would be compromised. The bank's relevant country director wrote:

> Regarding the load forecast for the Maharashtra market, the recent protracted discussions have led us to reconfirm CEA's 14th Electric Power Survey (EPS) as the most realistic forecast on which to base our analysis. As regards the important assumptions about the future performance of MSEB's existing system, we propose to reflect in our analysis the understandings reached during the processing of the Second Maharashtra Power Project in 1992 together with additional information obtained from and reviewed with MSEB subsequently. However, we cannot accept the more pessimistic scenario recently provided by MSEB according to which the existing system is projected to decline in efficiency...
>
> After extensive further review of the above parameters and detailed review of the analytical framework and the existing assumptions, we reconfirm our earlier conclusion that the Dabhol project as presently formulated is not economically justified and thus could not be financed by the Bank.[15]

At this point, it would have seemed sensible for the Indian government to reevaluate the project, but it forged ahead. Later, after it had examined the structure of the project and the correspondence among Enron, the government and the World Bank, the Munde Committee issued a scathing critique of the government's actions. The committee's report concluded:

> [T]he Central Government secured the services of the World Bank to assess the Enron Project. In fact, at one stage, Enron itself was seeking to involve the World Bank for finance and participation as, in the view of the then Chief Secretary, Maharashtra, "Enron is convinced that the World Bank has full and scientific knowledge of the working of the Power sector in India." This is despite the fact that the then Finance Secretary felt that Enron would pre-empt the other projects of the State

---

[15] Letter from Heinz Vergin, World Bank country director for India, to R. Vasudevan, secretary for the Indian Ministry of Power, July 26, 1993. Letter on file at Human Rights Watch.

from getting World Bank assistance, if Enron were allowed access to the World Bank funds. However, later in its Report, the World Bank clearly advised that the Enron Project is (i) unviable, (ii) does not satisfy the test of least cost power and (iii) is too large and (iv) is not justified by the power demands of Maharashtra. Once the World Bank's assessment came and it clearly vetoed the Project, the response of all those who persistently asked for the World Bank advice, confessing that in those areas the Government did not have experience or expertise, was to underplay and even suppress it. Almost every official other than the then Secretary of Finance supported the Project ignoring the World Bank's advice.[16]

By August 1993, another problem appeared for the government and the company: the Central Electricity Authority (CEA), which had questioned the project for some time. The CEA is the government body meant to oversee and regulate electricity generation throughout the country, and clearance from the CEA is mandatory for power projects to move forward.

The CEA's reservations about the capital costs were related to the payment structure between the MSEB and the company. The company's contract with the state was an "all-in-one" contract, meaning that all the costs of construction and operation would be covered by the tariff the company would charge the MSEB for electricity. The tariff amount was critically important: it would be the only payment made from the government to the company and, while the MSEB would be obliged to pay the company under the tariff, the costs would be passed on to consumers and other industries in the form of higher electricity prices. The tariff agreed upon, in the contract, specified a total payment (per the tariff) of $1.3-$1.4 billion a year for twenty years. The company would pay its costs of construction, operation, and other expenses from this amount, and the balance would be the company's profit. Consequently, the capital costs of the project were important for CEA to determine the rate of return for the company and whether the tariff was too high. Sometime in August, the CEA determined that the reasonable capital cost per kilowatt for a power project was less than half of Enron's price of electricity per kilowatt, meaning that electricity from the Dabhol project was more than twice as expensive as what the CEA found to be acceptable or competitive.[17]

---

[16] *Report of the Cabinet Sub-Committee...*, pp. 13-15.
[17] "Evaluation of the DESU (MCD) Bawana-GTCC Project by the Thermal Design Organization," Central Electricity Authority, August 1993. Letter on file at Human Rights Watch.

The price of the tariff, coupled with other reservations about the project, led the CEA to withhold its approval. Undeterred, the Maharashtra Industries, Energy and Labour Department asked the central government's Ministry of Energy to expedite clearance by the CEA.[18] In late August, Enron asked then Congress (I) Chief Minister of Maharashtra Sharad Pawar to pressure the CEA to approve the project. Enron's chief executive officer, Rebecca Mark, wrote:

Dear Mr. Pawar:

I understand from our people in Bombay and Delhi that we are making some progress with the Dabhol project approvals. However, it is still not clear when we can expect Cabinet approval and signing the Power Purchase Agreement. A key issue is clearance by CEA. Our people, together with MSEB, have met extensively with CEA this week to answer their questions about the project. The remaining concern seems to reside with Mr. Beg, Member Planning for Thermal Projects. He continues to hold up the project approval based upon the question of demand for power in Maharashtra. No one from the Ministry of Power in Delhi has given direction to Mr. Beg to move forward on this issue. Consequently, we have a project under the government's "fast track" program, approved by FIPB, but the CEA refuses to grant a clearance...

It is critical that we get the Power Purchase Agreement approved and signed now and that we start Phase I financing immediately. Because of GOM [Government of Maharashtra] delays in approval and the associated negative press of the last few weeks, the project is in danger. We are working on financing arrangements prior to project approval but the banks in India and externally are losing their enthusiasm based on lack of progress... We need to make immediate progress.[19]

The CEA granted an "in principle" clearance on September 20, 1993. This was done to allow Enron to finalize financing for the project. The final clearance

---

[18] Letter from N. Raghunathan, chief secretary, Maharashtra Department of Industries Energy and Labour, to R. Vasudevan, secretary, Department of Power, Ministry of Energy of the government of India, August 21, 1993. Letter on file at Human Rights Watch.

[19] Letter from Rebecca Mark, chief executive officer, Enron Power Development Corporation, to Sharad Pawar, chief minister of Maharashtra, August 26, 1993. Letter on file at Human Rights Watch.

was conditional on the company's obtaining other government permits from the Ministry of Environment and Forests and the Port Trust for construction of their harbor and port; and compliance with Section 29 of the Electricity (Supply) Act, 1948 (an issue discussed further below). The CEA also noted that the government of India should make certain policy decisions regarding the cost of importing liquefied natural gas, payments to the company, and the discrepancy between the Maharashtra government's estimate for the price of electricity and the central government's calculations.[20]

As noted by government officials during a Foreign Investment Promotion Board meeting on November 2, 1993, a key issue in the project was the price of power. They said that the CEA would examine the tariff and determine whether it was reasonable.[21] Two days later, in another meeting, the Ministry of Power said that the CEA would grant the clearance the week of November 8, 1993.[22]

On November 9, 1993, in a second examination into whether the costs of the project were justified, the CEA sent a letter detailing several questions to the Dabhol Power Corporation (DPC), asking for specific project costs to determine what the rate of return was for the company.

Initially, the CEA asked whether the project's construction costs had changed and whether the date of completion had changed, since the CEA's August 1993 analysis of the project. The company notified the CEA that costs and completion dates had changed but that this information was "irrelevant to CEA in this project because the tariff was guaranteed." The company argued that since the fees paid to the company were constant, regardless of capital costs, the company would lose money for a more expensive project and consequently bore the risk of increased costs, therefore it was unnecessary for the CEA to determine the costs.[23] The company's answers to the CEA's follow-up questions, in a November 10, 1993 letter from the DPC's director that was obtained by Human Rights Watch, were even more dismissive. A relevant portion of the letter reads as follows:

---

[20] Letter from V.V.R.K. Rao, secretary of the CEA, to the secretary of energy, government of Maharashtra, September 20, 1993. Letter on file at Human Rights Watch.

[21] Summary Record of the Foreign Investment Promotion Board meeting held on November 2, 1993. Record on file at Human Rights Watch.

[22] Summary Record of the Foreign Investment Promotion Board meeting held on November 5, 1993. Record on file at Human Rights Watch.

[23] Letter from Joseph Sutton, director, Dabhol Power Corporation, to Seth Vedantham, chief engineer, Central Electricity Authority, November 10, 1993. Letter on file at Human Rights Watch.

2. Please furnish the main items of equipment/systems/works separately for items furnished at page 8.1.
(i) plant and equipment
(ii) balance of plant and housing (item 4)
(iii) cargo, dock and harbor development
(iv) distillate/LNG [liquefied natural gas] facility (item 14)
(v) MSEB cost (item 14-1)

Response:
Your request for more detailed project costs of equipment/system/works other than those provided in the capital cost summary cannot be supported and is not deemed necessary. As mentioned earlier, the project assumes all capital cost risk and has agreed to a guaranteed tariff. Changes in capital cost are not passed on to the customer in the tariff.

3. From the cost estimates furnished at table 8.1, it is seen that the cost of balance of plant and equipment [is high]. The reasons for the high cost of balance of plant and housing may be furnished.

Response:
Same response as question #2 above.[24]

In effect, the Dabhol Power Corporation did not want to disclose its capital costs to the statutory body that was charged with reviewing the project for its cost-effectiveness, among other issues. The company argued (above) that it was unnecessary because with a fixed tariff that included the price of construction, the company would bear all the risks. However, as the Munde Committee report would note, capital costs have a direct impact on the tariff itself:

The most intriguing aspect of the Enron project has been the incredibly high capital cost of the Rs. 4.49 crores per megawatt [approximately $1.4 million per megawatt]. The previous Government and Enron have been justifying it on the basis that it compares well with the capital cost of the other Fast Track Projects cleared for the private sector. The

---

[24] Ibid.

comparative table of the capital cost of the seven Fast Track Projects is as under:

Project	Capacity (Megawatts)	Type of Fuel	Cost per Megawatt (Rupees in Crores)
Enron	2,015	Gas (LNG)	4.49
Jagrupadu	235	Gas	3.52
Godavari	208	Gas	3.60
Vishakapatnam	1,000	Coal	5.81
Mangalore	1,000	Coal	5.08
Ib Valley	420	Coal	4.82
Zero unit NLC	250	Lignite	4.50

It is evident from the above data that the cost of the Enron Project is more comparable to the coal based projects than to gas based projects. Even as compared to the other gas based projects the cost of the DPC Project is clearly higher by at least 25 percent. Considering the fact that the other gas based projects, Jagrupadu and Godavari, are insignificant in capacity as compared to Enron, a comparison with them will be misleading. Being small projects, their capital cost per megawatt is bound to be higher. Even then, the capital cost of the Enron project is higher than the cost per megawatt of these smaller projects...

In fact the high capital cost wiped out the main advantage that the Dabhol power was supposed to bring. Because gas based technology was to be used, the capital cost of the Project should have been much cheaper than a coal based plant, whereas the running cost would have been higher. In the instant case we have lost the advantage of a lower capital cost from a gas based plant while still retaining the disadvantages of a higher running cost.[25]

---

[25] *Report of the Cabinet Sub-Committee...*, pp. 25-27. One crore is equal to ten million rupees.

Background: New Delhi and Bombay 21

Most important, perhaps, was the committee's suspicion that a fixed tariff, under which the company paid all of its expenses, could provide an incentive for the company to negotiate a very high fixed tariff. The higher the tariff, the greater the profit for the company, derived from the margin between project expenses and total revenues. The Munde Committee reported:

> [P]rivate investors have a tendency to inflate costs which would finally lead to higher unit tariffs where the tariff structure is based on a cost plus approach. In a project like this where escalations have been built in and a guaranteed 90 percent offtake of power is assured, the incentive to inflate costs could well be imagined.[26]

Even though the company refused to provide important information to the CEA, the CEA did not hold up the project or contest the lack of cooperation. Instead, at a meeting of the Foreign Investment Promotion Board, the Ministry of Power sent a note informing the CEA that the finance secretary had found the cost of power to be in line with other projects.[27] At this juncture, the CEA apparently abdicated its statutory responsibilities to evaluate the project costs and tariffs and decided that, since the Ministry of Finance approved of the tariff, the CEA would not have to, even though the Ministry of Finance had no apparent authority to clear projects on CEA's behalf.[28] The matter ceased to be an issue; the CEA looked the other way.

On November 26, 1993, the CEA gave a provisional clearance to the project which would allow it to be finalized.[29] The government of Maharashtra took this provisional clearance as a final clearance and rushed to sign a final contract with Enron.[30] Within a week, the final contract, known as the Power Purchasing Agreement (PPA), was signed between the government of Maharashtra and the

---

[26] Ibid.

[27] Letter from R. Vasudevan, secretary, Ministry of Power, to Y.P. Gambhir, chairman, Central Electricity Authority, November 11, 1993. Letter on file at Human Rights Watch.

[28] Summary Record of Discussions of the 118th Meeting of the Central Electricity Authority on Techno-Economic Appraisal of Power Development Schemes, First Session, November 12, 1993. Record on file at Human Rights Watch.

[29] Letter from V.V.R.K. Rao, secretary Central Electricity Authority, to the Dabhol Power Corporation, November 26, 1993. Letter on file at Human Rights Watch.

[30] Note from U.K. Mukhopadhyay, energy secretary, to the secretary of the chief minister and principal secretary of the Finance Department, December 2, 1993. Note on file at Human Rights Watch.

Dabhol Power Corporation. The agreement finalized the "all in one" tariff structure in which the costs of construction and other costs would be covered through payments made by MSEB to the Dabhol Power Corporation.[31]

While the government and company had discussed and publicized the approximately $3 billion in foreign investment that would come to Maharashtra—the largest single foreign investment in India— to construct the project, they did not publicize the magnitude of the capital outflows from the government (through MSEB) to the company which were required to purchase Dabhol electricity. The numbers are staggering. According to a study by the Central Electricity Authority, the minimum amount MSEB would be required to pay for the proposed project was approximately $1.3 billion per year, or approximately $26 billion over the life of the twenty-year contract. The government would pay out, over twenty years, almost nine times what Enron would pay in. This price could increase if fuel costs, the costs of electricity transmission, or maintenance increased.[32]

The PPA authorized construction of the 695-megawatt Phase I and provided an option to build the larger Phase II. The agreement governed the purchase of electricity by the state (through the Maharashtra State Electricity Board) from the company. The PPA formalized the "all inclusive" tariff.

One item of particular concern to some officials was that the tariff paid to the company was denominated in U.S. dollars. Since the Indian rupee is not fully convertible, the government must pay in the rupee equivalent of U.S. dollars in order to make a dollar-based payment. However, if the rupee is devalued against the dollar, the amount the government pays increases. For example, when the PPA was signed, one dollar was equal to thirty-two rupees. At the time of this writing, one dollar equals about forty rupees. In terms of the tariff agreement, the cost of power, in rupees, has increased by 20 percent because of currency fluctuations. This problem was acknowledged as early as 1993 by the Foreign Investment Promotion Board:

> Finance Secretary stated that there had been some criticism regarding the high cost of power from this project. It was necessary that the Government of India and the State Government satisfy themselves that the cost of power is more or less the same as the cost of similar projects

---

[31] Summary Record of Discussions of the 118th Meeting of the Central Electricity Authority.

[32] Financial and Economic Appraisal of Dabhol Combined Cycle Power Project by the Central Electricity Authority, November 1993. Report on file at Human Rights Watch.

which would come up in 1997. An additional concern in this case would arise because the tariff was denominated in U.S. dollars and therefore apart from the escalation in dollar terms, account would need to be taken of the expected depreciation rate in the Indian rupee.[33]

Concern over the tariff was also noted in the 1995 Munde Committee report. The Munde Committee was even more critical of the dollar-denominated tariff than the Foreign Investment Promotion Board and noted:

> The most amazing aspect of the entire Project is the fact that the tariff for power has been denominated in U.S. dollars. This means that, regardless of the fluctuations in the dollar-rupee exchange rate, the Project will always earn the same amount. In other words, they are permanently insulated from the vagaries of exchange rate fluctuations. The Sub-Committee can see no reason whatsoever for this... In no other case...is the entrepreneur protected against fluctuations in the international currency market.[34]

While the company insulated itself from currency fluctuations, the state could not. The consumer of the company's electricity was the Maharashtra State Electricity Board (MSEB). The MSEB, as with all the state electricity boards in the country, was in poor financial shape, and its debt load was quickly increasing. For example, as early as 1993, the state government's Department of Industries, Energy, and Labour knew the MSEB might not be able to pay for the Dabhol power:

> The other important issue is the financial position of MSEB itself. Even under the existing conditions, MSEB has to borrow from the State Government and other financial institutions at increasing rates of interest to finance all its development plans. As per the current projection MSEB's interest burden is going up at a fast pace. The burden was Rs. 436 crores [about $136 million in 1993] in 1990-91, Rs 552 crores [$172 million at the 1994 conversion rate], Rs 650 crores [$203 million] in 1992-93, and Rs. 788 crores [$246 million] in 1993-

---

[33] Summary Record of the Foreign Investment Promotion Board (FIPB) Meeting Held on November 2, 1993. Record on file at Human Rights Watch.

[34] *Report of the Cabinet Sub-Committee...*, pp. 29-30.

94. The interest burden has almost doubled in five years. Even if the generation projects come up in the private sector, MSEB will find it difficult to generate internal resources for improvement of the transmission system.[35]

In order for the company to agree to the project it demanded insurance that the debt-ridden MSEB would not default on its payments. Insurance, in this case, took the form of a "counter-guarantee" by the state of Maharashtra. This agreement would compel the state government to pay the company's fees if the MSEB were unable to meet its financial commitments. The agreement guaranteed the company a steady income for the life of the PPA, regardless of demand. Furthering the surety, the state government waived sovereign immunity in the counter-guarantee. This meant that if the Maharashtra state government were unable to pay the company, the company could potentially seize any state assets in repayment of arrears.[36]

Moreover, the central government extended a similar counter-guarantee in the event that the state of Maharashtra defaulted on its payments to Enron. A counter-guarantee was signed on September 9, 1994 by the government of India, which by

---

[35] Additional views of the Finance Department of the Maharashtra Department of Industries, Energy and Labour regarding Enron Power Project, August 1993. Memorandum on file at Human Rights Watch. The dollar amounts are based on the 1993 conversion rate of thirty-two rupees to on U.S. dollar.

[36] Guarantee of the State of Maharashtra to the Dabhol Power Corporation, signed by U.K. Mukhopadhyay, secretary of energy, and Joseph Sutton, director the Dabhol Power Corporation, February 10, 1994. Guarantee on file at Human Rights Watch. The relevant clause of the counter-guarantee states: (E) Sovereign Immunity: The Guarantor unconditionally and irrevocably: (1) agrees that the execution, delivery and performance by it of this Guarantee constitute private and commercial acts rather than public or governmental acts; (2) agrees that, should any proceedings be brought against it or its assets in any jurisdiction in relation to this Guarantee or any transaction contemplated by this Guarantee, no immunity from such proceedings shall, to the extent that it would otherwise be entitled to do so under the laws of India, be claimed by or on behalf of itself or with respect to its assets; (3) waives any right of immunity which it or any of its assets now has or may acquire in the future in any jurisdiction; and (4) consents generally in respect of the enforcement of any judgement against it in any such proceedings in any jurisdiction to the giving of any relief or the issue of any process in connection with such proceedings (including, without limitation, the making, enforcement or execution against or in respect of any property whatsoever of its use or intended use).

separate action also waived sovereign immunity.[37] (Another party interested in counter-guarantees was the U.S. government. Then-Secretary of Energy Hazel O' Leary, on an official visit to India, reportedly said, "We are very happy that the first project with Enron has received a counter-guarantee..." at a meeting with the Confederation of Indian Industry.[38] We discuss the promotional efforts of the U.S. government in Section VIII below.)

Political Opposition to the Project

While negotiations between the company and the government reached the point of project implementation, opposition parties, namely the Shiv Sena and the BJP—both Hindu nationalist parties—were vocally criticizing the agreement on the grounds that it was fraught with corruption, was not in the best interests of the state, and pandered to multinational corporations, whose involvement in India these parties generally opposed. The controversial project thus remained in the spotlight.

In 1994, as the DPC set up operations in Maharashtra and began to come into contact with the local population, the controversy became acute in the communities directly affected. (See below)

On July 7, 1994, Ramdas Nayak, a member of the BJP, filed a High Court case against the Indian government and the Dabhol Power Corporation on the grounds that projects in "core sectors" should not be implemented without transparency and competitive bidding, and that the counter guarantees violated provisions in the Indian constitution that regulate government borrowing. The suit sought to cancel the PPA and the counter-guarantees between the government and the DPC. The case, however, was dismissed on August 8, 1994.[39]

The Shiv Sena and BJP sought to harness popular opposition to the project in order to win control of the Maharashtra state government. Opposition candidates promised that they would review the project and accused the Congress (I) government, led by Sharad Pawar, of corruption, lack of transparency and operating against the public interest. The Enron issue, combined with the Shiv Sena-BJP strategy of accusing the Pawar government of not adequately addressing the Bombay riots and Bombay bomb blasts and of siding with Muslims, eventually won the Shiv Sena-BJP coalition control of the Maharashtra government.

---

[37] Guarantee of the government of India to the Dabhol Power Corporation, September 4, 1994. Guarantee on file at Human Rights Watch.

[38] "Secretary O'Leary Hosts First Reunion with India," press release by the United States Department of Energy, September 28, 1994.

[39] *Center for Indian Trade Unions and Others vs. Union of India and Others*, Special Leave Petition Number 7734 of 1997.

The Munde Committee Report

Upon their election in March 1995, the new government under Chief Minister Manohar Joshi announced that it would review the Dabhol Power project.[40] A committee chaired by Deputy Chief Minister Gopinath Munde—the "Sub-Committee to Review the Dabhol Power Project"—was constituted on May 3, 1995.[41] The committee undertook a comprehensive study of the project, reviewing thousands of pages of documents and interviewing representatives of numerous organizations concerned with the issue, including the company itself.

We have cited this report and many of the same sources extensively, in describing the background of the project. We have detailed the committee's findings regarding the price of the tariff, the financial impact of the project, and the manner in which the former government negotiated the deal. The committee had other findings as well. It examined issues related to corruption, namely the lack of competitive bidding, lack of transparency, secrecy of negotiations, and whether the company received any "undue concessions." The committee's conclusions follow:

> 1. On the question of competitive bids:
> The previous Government has committed a grave impropriety by resorting to private negotiations on a one on one basis with Enron and under circumstances which made the Enron/MSEB arrangement on Dabhol to lack transparency. Although there was no policy formulated for competitive bidding in power projects this has been accepted practice, in the larger public interest, to involve more than one contender. There was no compelling reason not to involve a second contender for Dabhol. Actually, such a thought does not seem to have occurred to anyone at all. Therefore the Sub-Committee strongly disapproves of the one to one negotiations with Enron and is clearly of the view that it violates standard and well-tested norms of propriety for public organisations.
>
> 2. On whether there was any secret or off the record negotiations:
> Considering the records available with the State Government and the MSEB, we are led to the irresistible conclusion that they are not the only guide to what actually happened. It is reasonably clear that several

---

[40] "Indian State Says Will Review Enron Project," Reuters, March 14, 1995.
[41] *Report of the Cabinet Sub-Committee...*, pp. 1-3.

unseen factors and forces seem to have worked to get Enron what it wanted.

3. On whether the capital cost of the Project is reasonable:
On the basis of the material accessed by the Sub-Committee, it concludes that the capital cost of the DPC project was inflated.

4. On whether undue favours and concessions have been given for the Project:
Several unusual features of the negotiations and final agreement have been pointed out by the Sub-Committee in the report which makes it clear that whatever Enron wanted was granted without demur.

5. Whether the rate for power from the Dabhol plant is reasonable:
The Sub-Committee is of the view that because of the denomination of tariff for power in U.S. dollars and other reasons, the consumer will have to pay a much higher price for power than is justified. This is clearly not reasonable.

6. On the environmental aspects of the Project:
The Sub-Committee is of the view that the real environmental issue is whether such a huge power project should be located in such an unpolluted part of Maharashtra and whether there is any other part of the State where it could have been located. Also whether a project of lesser size could help the preservation of the environment better was not gone into. It is evident from the environmental assessment that marine life and plants may have to face problems if adequate care is not taken.

7. On whether the Project is useful to the State:
The Sub-Committee is of the view that such high cost power as Enron envisages will, in the immediate future, and in the long run, adversely affect Maharashtra and the rapid industrialization of the State and its competitiveness.[42]

Based on these findings, the committee concluded:

---

[42] Ibid., pp. 37-40.

> [T]he arrangement in force is not tenable because of the infirmities pointed out above in the terms and conditions of the contract. It, therefore, recommends that Phase II of the Project should be canceled and Phase I should be repudiated. [sic][43]

This outcome was stunning: the committee recommended cancellation of the largest single foreign investment in India. Its grounds were corruption, lack of transparency, the high costs associated with the project, and the lack of benefit to the state.

Chief Minister Manohar Joshi announced that Phase I would be stopped and Phase II would be canceled on August 3, 1995.[44] In a speech to the Maharashtra legislature, Joshi said:

> This agreement is an anti-Maharashtra agreement. This agreement is mindless and devoid of self-respect and to accept this agreement as it is shall amount to cheating the public. This agreement can never be called an agreement and therefore, it is important to uphold the self-respect and interest of Maharashtra by canceling this agreement even if that results in some financial burden.[45]

Following the announcement to cease construction, Enron initiated arbitration proceedings against the Maharashtra government in the United Kingdom during August 1995. The company stated that it wanted to recoup up to $600 million in costs because the contract was suspended but also stated that it was willing to renegotiate the PPA.[46]

Countering the company's actions, the Maharashtra government filed a court case in the Bombay High Court against the MSEB and DPC in September 1995. Both the lawsuit and the government's stance in arbitration proceedings contended that the contract with Enron was contrary to the public interest and conceived through corruption. The government argued that, in these circumstances, the PPA

---

[43] Ibid., p. 40.

[44] Mark Nicholson, " Indian State Scraps U.S. Group's Power Project," *Financial Times*, August 4, 1995.

[45] The government of Maharashtra's translation of the chief minister's statement in the Maharashtra Assembly, August 7, 1995. Statement on file at Human Rights Watch.

[46] Jeremy Clift, "Enron Seeks Arbitration in $2.8 Billion India Deal," Reuters, August 7, 1995; Feizal Samath, "U.S. Enron Corp Offers Fresh India Power Deal," Reuters, August 31, 1995.

should be declared void and related contracts such as the counter-guarantees should be void as well.[47] Arguing as to why the contract should be voided, the state government's lawyers stated:

> In the proceedings in the High Court of Bombay, it is alleged that payments were made by the claimant in these arbitrations by way of illegal bribes. A contract which involves the bribery of a public official or officer is a contract procured by commission of a criminal offence. Not only is the making of a bribe a criminal offence, it also means that the officers and agents of the Maharashtra State Electricity Board ("MSEB") who purported to contract on behalf of the board were exceeding their authority. An employee or agent has no authority to bind his principal to a fraudulent transaction. The consequence of this is that the MSEB were not contractually bound by the actions of their employees or agents purportedly on their behalf. This means that the MSEB never entered into the PPA. It was an agreement made by officers without authority to act. It therefore, does not bind the MSEB.[48]

On November 1, Enron officials apologized to the Maharashtra state government and offered a "renegotiated" project.[49] The government, specifically the unelected leader of the Shiv Sena, Bal Thackeray, announced that the "Enron people have accepted nearly all our conditions."[50] However, the arbitration proceedings were not resolved, so the project remained in limbo.

The "Renegotiated" Project

On January 8, 1996, in a complete reversal of its earlier stance and its claims in a lawsuit and arbitration proceedings, the Shiv Sena-BJP government in Maharashtra announced that it would accept a "renegotiated" project. The

---

[47] *State of Maharashtra vs. Dabhol Power Company and others*, Civil Writ Petition Number 3392 of 1995 in the Bombay High Court.

[48] Notes of arbitration proceedings between the government of Maharashtra and the Dabhol Power Corporation written by Christopher Carr and R.J. McGrane, lawyers for the government of Maharashtra, November 2, 1995, p. 7. Notes on file at Human Rights Watch.

[49] "Enron Bosses Apologise to India State Chief," Reuters, November 1, 1995.

[50] Clarence Fernandez, "Indian Leader Seems to Give Axed Enron Thumbs Up," Reuters, November 1, 1995. Bal Thackeray, founder and current leader of the Shiv Sena party is widely acknowledged as the final arbiter in Maharashtra government decisions despite the fact that he is not an elected government official and has never held public office.

government said that it had cut the capital costs from $2.8 billion to approximately $2.5 billion and had reduced the tariff by 22.5 percent.[51] According to several observers, the reported savings of 22.5 percent were actually not made on Phase I at all. The reduction was based on the projected costs of Phase II. In other words, the Shiv Sena-BJP government signed an agreement to build Phase II when the previous government's agreement with the DPC made Phase II optional. Then the Shiv Sena government reported it had saved 22.5 percent on Phase II, thereby reducing costs. It failed to mention that the former agreement had no obligation to Phase II. Costs for Phase I are the same as the old agreement, and all the savings are on Phase II.

The renegotiated project was excoriated in the Indian business press. For example, after reviewing the renegotiated deal, a major Indian financial newspaper, *Business Line,* noted:

> The new terms recommended by the six-member Negotiating Group set up by the Maharashtra Government to revive the Dabhol Power Project are unacceptably advantageous to Enron and clearly disadvantageous to Maharashtra and India. Notwithstanding the cost reductions advertised for Phase II of a 2,450 MW power plant in an exercise which smacks of disingenuousness and technical and financial sophistry, the revised terms are open to all the core objections that were successfully raised against the original deal...
>
> In one vital respect, the attempted cure will make the situation worse for the Maharashtra State Electricity Board than it might have been with the original Power Purchase Agreement. That was before the Shiv Sena-BJP government (at Bal Thackeray's diktat) decided to go back on a major election promise and revive the "scandalous" and "corrupt" Enron deal on renegotiated terms. The 1993 PPA covered only Phase I, which meant that Maharashtra would have been saddled with an extortionate 695 MW plant functioning as a baseload station...
>
> The revised package, which is before the State Government and approval, saddles the MSEB with a telescoped Phase I and Phase II of an expanded power plant. In essence, what the numbers provided by the

---

[51] Mark Nicholson, "Delhi Clears Way for $2.5bn Dabhol Power Plant," *Financial Times,* July 10, 1996.

expert Negotiating Group ask us to buy is lower unit cost created by economies of larger-scale production—the terms of which are still one-sided and go against rational economic considerations. [52]

Having reported this savings, the government committed itself (and consumers) to finance the construction of a Phase I that was expanded to 740 megawatts and a 1,320-megawatt Phase II. The previous agreement, that the Shiv Sena-BJP government renegotiated, had only committed the government to the 695-megawatt Phase I and gave the government the option to authorize Phase II. In effect, the government had agreed to a project of approximately 2,100 megawatts—almost three times its original capacity. Rebecca Mark, the CEO of the Enron Power Development Corporation, announced that construction would commence within ninety days.[53]

The CITU Lawsuit

The drastic change in the government's position was not lost on the Indian public, and on April 8, 1996, the Center for Indian Trade Unions (CITU) and an energy analyst, Abhay Mehta, filed a public interest litigation against the government and the company.[54] The petition alleged that the reported clearances required for the project were not obtained; that since the project had been renegotiated, it had to obtain new licenses and clearances; and that "having charged the Dabhol Power Company and Enron with fraud, misrepresentation, corruption and bribery, it was not open to the Government of Maharashtra to negotiate and purport to contract with the said DPC/Enron."[55] Vivek Monteiro, a representative of the CITU, told Human Rights Watch the justification for the writ petition:

> The CITU/Abhay Mehta petition in the Bombay High Court challenged the project on economic issues. Namely that it was unsustainable, violated laws in many ways, obtained government clearances by submitting unfeasible or fraudulent documents. It is a complex

---

[52] "Enron: An Indefensible Exercise," *Business Line*, December 12, 1995.

[53] Mark Nicholson, "Dabhol Plant Finally Gets Green Light," *Financial Times*, January 9, 1996.

[54] This was the last of fourteen court cases filed against the project by various individuals, NGOs, and political parties. All of the previous cases were dismissed.

[55] *Center For Indian Trade Unions and others vs. The Union of India and Others*, Special Leave Petition filed in the Supreme Court, p. B.

technical matter. CITU was concerned about the high cost of power associated with the project.[56]

The petitioners' first problem was an inability to obtain counsel for the petition. According to Monteiro, "It was hard to find a lawyer because Enron had retained or briefed every major lawyer in Bombay."[57] Representing the plaintiffs would thus be a conflict of interest. Finally, the petitioners obtained the services of Sunip Sen, a commercial lawyer practicing in the Bombay High Court. Sen told us:

> I got involved because they found me. Apparently Enron placed all the leading lawyers in Delhi and Bombay on retainer, so the petitioners could not find representation. I am a commercial lawyer and did not really do public interest litigation. I like to stay neutral and do not want to be seen by the court as just a public interest lawyer.[58]

After five days of oral arguments, the case was accepted on April 26, 1996 by Justice B.N. Srikrishna, a well-known judge who had led the investigation into the role of the Shiv Sena and BJP during the Bombay riots in 1992-1993.[59]

The same day that Justice Srikrishna accepted the case, the lawyers for Enron petitioned the chief justice of the High Court, M.B. Shah, to expedite the case and transfer it from Srikrishna to a two-judge division bench, whose ruling could not be appealed. The rationale for the petition was that every day, the company was losing approximately $269,000 because work had stopped.[60] Less than a week later, on May 2, an administrative order was issued, stating that the chief justice had ordered all public interest litigations to be given to division benches.[61] Sen, the plaintiffs' lawyer, told us:

---

[56] Human Rights Watch interview with Vivek Monteiro, Bombay, January 28, 1998.
[57] Ibid.
[58] Human Rights Watch interview with Sunip Sen, Bombay, February 4, 1998.
[59] For more information on the Srikrishna investigation and the Bombay riots, see "India: Communal Violence and the Denial of Justice," *a Human Rights Watch Short Report*, April 1996. Justice Srikrishna released his report into the riots in February 1998. The report was more than 700 pages long and indicted leaders of the Shiv Sena in promoting violence against Muslims.
[60] Human Rights Watch interview with Sunip Sen.
[61] Hutokshi Rustomfram, "Pulling the Rug to Spread the Carpet: The Enron Litigation," *The Lawyers Collective*, Bombay, November 1996, p. 7.

> The chief justice cannot transfer the case to a division bench; the case would first have to be referred to the chief justice by Srikrishna, which it was not. This was clearly interference by Shah through administration of a judicial order. A High Court judge's decision can only be reversed by an appeal, which did not happen. A High Court order cannot be changed by legislation, either. There are plenty of Supreme Court rulings on this. This was blatantly irregular.[62]

Vivek Monteiro also recalled the incident and told Human Rights Watch:

> Initially, Justice Srikrishna got the case and accepted the petition. The same evening, Enron's lawyers go to the chief justice, M.B. Shah, and lobby to have the case transferred to [the two-judge panel of Justices] Seraf and Rane. Enron claimed that if Srikrishna hears the case, it will cost Enron 86 lakhs per day in project costs, but when the case was transferred, they dropped this argument. It is very uncommon to have a case switched like that. It is extremely rare, basically unheard of, for a chief justice to overrule a High Court judge without conducting a separate hearing on the matter.[63]

The order to transfer public interest litigations to a division bench created an uproar among High Court lawyers. Initially, lawyers considered appealing the decision to the court, but they declined to do so for various reasons: the court was on a five-week recess, and challenging the chief justice would have ramifications on future cases.

The case was transferred to Justices B.P. Seraf and M.S. Rane. On June 3, the two-judge court told the petitioners that they could amend their petition so that the court could examine all the aspects of the project: alleged corruption, the price of power, the lack of transparency, and whether the company had obtained the proper clearances and licenses for the project. CITU regarded this as evidence that Justice Seraf was positively disposed toward their petition, according to Sen.[64]

Justice Seraf gave the petitioners three days to amend their petition. The plaintiffs submitted their amended petition on June 6. The lawyers for the Dabhol Power Corporation, however, asked for three weeks to reply to the petition, which

---

[62] Human Rights Watch interview with Sunip Sen.
[63] Human Rights Watch interview with Vivek Monteiro.
[64] Human Rights Watch interview with Sunip Sen.

was granted by Seraf. In early July, the lawyers for the government of Maharashtra asked for more time, and a hearing was set for the end of July.[65]

Following the petitioners' submission of the amended petition, Seraf ruled that because all the old issues were raised, the case was barred by *res judicata*. Although it was Justice Seraf who had asked that the petition be amended, he said on the record that the request came from Sen. According to Sen, Justice Seraf also asked Sen not to argue corruption but then said the plaintiffs chose not to argue corruption and therefore, had provided no evidence of it. When Seraf heard the case, he also barred more than 1,200 pages of the evidence that the plaintiffs had submitted to support their allegations. As a result of this ruling, the evidence—more than 1,200 pages—could never be used against the government or the company in any future Indian court case because Seraf had barred it under *res judicata*.[66]

The government's position was particularly weak on the corruption issue. The government had previously filed a suit against the company and had engaged in arbitration on the grounds that the contract with the company was illegal because bribery had been used to secure the contract. During the CITU case, however, the government reversed its position and claimed it had no evidence of corruption and had only raised the issue to extract concessions from the company. The petitioners argued that this statement amounted to an admission of prior perjury, since the government had initiated court and arbitration proceedings alleging corruption and was now in another judicial proceeding claiming to have lied about those allegations.

Ultimately, on December 12, 1996, Justices Seraf and Rane dismissed the petition on the grounds that the information was old; that the petitioners had waited too long to file their case; and that this agreement was outside the purview of judicial scrutiny. They refused to rule on the perjury or corruption issues, thereby avoiding a ruling on the government's credibility or on the larger issue of whether officials had been influenced through bribery. Along with the toothless ruling, however, Seraf and Rane issued a scathing critique of the government. Seraf and Rane wrote:

> [W]e do find that the statement of the State Government made before this court to the effect that corruption was never alleged by it at any time except in the plaint in the suit and in the submissions before the

---

[65] "Pulling the Rug to Spread the Carpet...," p. 7.
[66] Human Rights Watch interview with Sunip Sen.

arbitrators is factually not correct. We have once again glanced through the Munde Committee report and the speech of the Chief Minister to verify the above claim. We find enough indications in the Munde Committee report which suggest corruption by those who were responsible for the deal and the PPA...

The message of corruption, bribery and fraud is eloquent in the above statements. We are really amazed at the bald statements made by the Government in support of its actions from time to time. When it wanted to scrap the project and decided to scrap it, it boldly said everything which it felt necessary to support the same. It talked of lack of competitive bidding and transparency, the speed and haste in finalising the project. It also condemned those who were responsible for the deal. It went to the extent of filing suit in this Court and made all possible statements and allegations it thought necessary to get the PPA declared null and void by the Court. It worked the same way when it wanted to stall the arbitration proceedings. But once it decided to revive the project, it acted in the very same manner in which its predecessors in office had done. It forgot all about competitive bidding and transparency. The only transparency it claims is the constitution of the negotiating team. The speed with which the negotiating group studied the project, made a proposal for renegotiation which was accepted by Dabhol, and submitted its report is unprecedented...The Committee, we are told, examined the project, collected data on various similar other projects as well as internal bids including data on a similar project executed by Enron in the U.K., held considerable negotiations, settled the terms of revival of the project, got the consent of Enron...and submitted its exhaustive report along with data and details to the Government of Maharashtra on 19th November, 1995, just 11 days after its formation...The speed at which the whole thing was done by the negotiating group is unprecedented. What would stop someone today, as was said by the Chief Minister in the context of the original PPA, "Enron revisited, Enron saw and Enron conquered—much more than what it did earlier."

However, we need not go into all those aspects because that is outside the scope and ambit of the powers of judicial review... As indicated earlier, it is not within the domain of this Court in exercise of its power of judicial review to examine the merits of the Government. That will amount to sitting in appeal over governmental decision which is not permissible... In any event, one thing that is obvious is that at every stage, it is the common man who has been taken for a ride during elections by the Shiv Sena-BJP alliance by making Enron an election issue and a part of its election manifesto and after coming into power, by reviewing the project and branding it as anti-Maharashtra, anti-people, alleging corruption, bribery, fraud, etc., by scrapping the same and telling the people that the promise made to them to scrap the project had been fulfilled. When the government decided to revive the same, it came out with a different statement that it had succeeded in snatching some concessions from Enron.[67]

The court also criticized Enron/DPC for its conduct throughout the process. Continually, the company claimed that it had been unjustly maligned while it was providing a service to the Indian people and was forced to spend millions of dollars "educating" Indian officials and the public on the merits of the project. In response to these claims, the court stated:

We have also given our careful consideration to the submissions... that Enron has been victimised for no fault of its own. We are, however, of the opinion that to some extent, "Enron" is also responsible for vitiating the atmosphere and for the anti-Enron campaign. In our opinion, the multinationals who want to invest in developing countries should not indulge in tall talks about educating the people of those countries. The decision of multinationals to invest in that country is based on the security of its investment and lucrative returns on the same. It is not activated by the desire to help the resource-starved nations. They do no charity. They move out of their country for greener pastures or better returns. They should, therefore, act and behave like an investor or an industrial house and not as a Government.[68]

In the end, none of the issues that formed the basis of opposition to the project were adjudicated in the courts. The project, although suspended for eight months, was allowed to start construction. The petitioners, dissatisfied with Seraf's ruling,

---

[67] Judgement of Justice B.P. Seraf and M.S. Rane on Writ Petition 2456 of 1996, *Center for Indian Trade Unions and Others vs. Union of India and others*.
[68] Ibid.

filed a "Special Leave Petition" with the Supreme Court of India in an attempt to appeal. The court accepted the petition but ruled that it would only look into the conduct of the state government and would not examine the agreement between the company and the central government or allegations of corruption. At the time of this writing, that case is still pending.

Without any judicial or governmental recourse, the public, specifically those organizations and individuals opposed to the project and the manner in which it was negotiated and implemented, expressed their opposition to the company through protests in the district where the project was located (See Section V). The state, in turn, committed human rights violations to suppress opposition to the project. In this context, a statement in Seraf and Rane' final ruling was particularly telling:

> This case has highlighted to the people as to how, even after 50 years of independence, political considerations outweigh the public interest and the interest of the State and to what extent the Government can go to justify its actions.[69]

---

[69] Judgement of Justice B.P. Seraf and M.S. Rane on Writ Petition 2456 of 1996.

III. Background to the Protests: Ratnagiri District

Local opposition to the Dabhol Power project stems from the same issues that made it controversial at the outset—allegations of corruption, lack of transparency, lack of competitive bidding, and the high cost of the tariff—and, in addition, a series of issues directly affecting the livelihoods of local people and the degradation of the local environment. Professor Sadanand Pawar is a recognized local leader of the opposition to the Dabhol Power project. He is an economics professor in Bombay, who is from Pawarsakari village—about six kilometers from the DPC site. Pawar, who was arrested and harassed on several occasions due to his opposition and participation in protests against the project (see below), explained the impact of the high cost of power and corruption at the local level:

> People say we are opposed to power projects; this is basically wrong. We are opposed to the pricing of power and the project. We would be for a good power project. It [the project tariff] is linked to dollars. Forty years ago, four rupees equaled one dollar. When the PPA was signed, thirty-two rupees equaled one dollar. Today, thirty-eight to forty rupees equals one dollar. Since the contract forces the state to pay in dollars, the price of Enron power will be one of the most expensive... Pricing of electricity determines which industries will enter nearby areas. With Enron's tariff, only chemical industries can survive—which will destroy the environment and survival of people. Engineering, electrical, and heavy industries cannot afford to pay the price charged by Enron. What we are afraid of is that the area, post-Enron, will be a chemical zone... It could be another Bhopal in the making.[70]

Coupled with the deal-making process, land acquisition and environmental degradation are at the center of local concerns and opposition to the project. Human Rights Watch does not have the expertise to assess environmental concerns, but we note that environmental degradation is a major cause of opposition to energy projects around the world, and the subsequent human rights violations that take place are inappropriate responses to individuals seeking to preserve or improve their environment.

---

[70] Human Rights Watch interview with Professor Sadanand Pawar, Bombay, February 16, 1998.

The area surrounding the Dabhol Power project consists of several *talukas* (groups of villages) comprising the agricultural villages of Aareygon, Borbatlewadi, Katalwadi, Nagewadi, Pawarsakari, and Ranavi and the fishing villages Anjanvel and Veldur. These communities, home to more than 92,000 people, are wholly dependent on natural resources.[71] According to the Center for Holistic Studies, a Bombay-based nongovernmental organization that specializes in research and documentation, the Dabhol Power project would produce large-scale displacement and economic disruption in the surrounding villages. Citing the DPC's own environmental impact assessment— conducted by the Bombay-based firm, Associated Industrial Consultants—the Center for Holistic Studies reported that the project would displace approximately 2,000 people. The DPC's consultants had also estimated that land acquisition for the project and the environmental impact of construction and operation would affect at least 92,000 people, that is, the entire populations of the villages named above.[72]

On March 12, 1993, during a meeting between Enron officials and the state government, a discussion took place about the project's land requirements and its impact on local communities. According to the minutes of the meeting, the government decided to begin acquiring land after consultations with the company, but not the public. The minutes state:

> Mr. Bobby Farris, General Manager, Enron, indicated that a suitable development plan is still to be worked out. However, approximately 400 hectares of land will be required for the plant...
>
> Mr. Bobby Farris informed that as storage of LNG [Liquefied Natural Gas] tankers are involved, shifting of residents of Veldur as well as Anjanvel villages may be necessary. Chairman requested the District Collector to identify the suitable site for rehabilitation of the people...
>
> Chairman (MSEB) requested MIDC to go ahead with the process of land acquisition and arrangements for fresh water as well as construction water...Chairman, MSEB and Mr. Joe Sutton, Vice

---

[71] Center for Holistic Studies, "Enron: The Power to Do It All," *Indranet Journal* (Bombay), Vol. 3, No. 2-4, 1994, pp. 10-11.
[72] Ibid.

President, Enron Power Development Corporation, thanked the participants.[73]

Following the agreement between the company and the government to acquire land and water, the company was legally required to post a notice in newspapers stating that it was constructing a power plant and that it would entertain any inquiries or complaints for a two month period following the publication of the announcement. This requirement is part of the Electricity (Supply) Act, 1948.[74] The company's announcement states:

> Any licensee or any other person interested in taking objection, if any, in respect of the above scheme may please make representation to that effect within two months from the date of publication of this Notification. Any representation received after two months shall not be entertained. The representation or concerned correspondence in this regard, may please be addressed to the Chief Engineer, Dabhol Power Company, "Nirmal" 17th floor, Nariman Point, Bombay 400 021. For any additional information on the above Schemes, please write on the above address.[75]

---

[73] Minutes of the meeting between government officers and Enron held on 12.3.93 at MSEB's Head Office to discuss about the Dabhol Power Project, transcribed March 26, 1993, pp. 3-4. Minutes of meeting on file at Human Rights Watch.

[74] Section 29(1) and Section 29 (2) of the Electricity (Supply) Act, 1948, state: **Submission of schemes for concurrence of Authority, etc.**—(1) Every scheme estimated to involve a capital expenditure exceeding such sum, as may be fixed by the Central Government, from time to time, by notification in the official gazette, shall, as soon as may be after it is prepared, be submitted to the Authority for its concurrence. (2) Before finalisation of any scheme of the nature referred to in sub-section (1) and the submission thereof to the Authority for concurrence, the Board or, as the case may be, the generating company shall cause such scheme, which among other things shall contain the estimates of the capital expenditure involved, salient features thereof and the benefits that may accrue therefrom, to be published in the official gazette of the State concerned and in such local newspapers as the Board or the generating company may consider necessary along with a notice date, not being less than two months after the date of such publications, before which licensees and other persons interested may make representations on such scheme.

[75] Letter of Public Notification written by the chief engineer of the Dabhol Power Corporation, Bombay, September 21, 1993. Letter on file at Human Rights Watch.

The notification was published in local papers on September 21, 1993. On November 21, 1993, the last day the company was required to entertain letters of inquiry or complaint, the Dabhol Power Corporation sent a letter to the government of Maharashtra's undersecretary of energy, stating that they had complied with the act. This was detailed in a letter from the undersecretary of energy to the Central Electricity Authority:

> Please find enclosed a letter from M/s Enron in which they have said that they have not received any objections pursuant to the publication of the Notification about the proposed Dabhol Power Project. It would, therefore, appear that the requirements of Section 29 of the Electricity (Supply) Act have been met.[76]

The company's statement to the government—if correctly reflected in the official correspondence—was entirely misleading. The company had in fact received thirty-four complaints and queries from NGOs, journalists, local residents whose land had been acquired, and government officials within the statutorily defined two-month period (September 21 to November 21, 1993).[77] Several individuals informed the company that their land was bulldozed, ruining their crops, and requested that the company stop acquiring land from them.

The company's response to villagers' letters reinforced criticism about the project's lack of transparency. DPC chose not to provide specific responses to the letters. Instead of detailed information, the company issued a form letter stating that the villagers' inquiries would be looked into and that there would be no negative impacts on the area.[78] The district collector, the most senior government official in the district, was also unaware of the company's activities and sent a letter himself asking for more information about the project.

Many of the local residents' letters to DPC requested more information about the project in order for local organizations and individuals to determine whether the project was beneficial for the community. For example, this excerpt is from a letter written by Yashwant Bait, then *Mandal* (the village-level government)

---

[76] Letter from the undersecretary of energy of the Maharashtra state government, U.K. Mukhopadhyay, to the Central Electricity Authority, November 23, 1993. Letter on file at Human Rights Watch.

[77] These letters are on file at Human Rights Watch.

[78] Letter from the Dabhol Power Corporation to Sharish V. Deshpande, November 1993. Letter on file at Human Rights Watch.

secretary for the villages of Anjanvel, Borbatlewadi, Katalwadi, Ranavi, and Veldur, to the Dabhol Power Corporation:

> [T]he government of Maharashtra has approved [the] Dabhol thermal power project in [the] villages [of] Anjanvel, Ranavi and Veldur in Guhagar Taluka... In [the] Maharashtra Times, dated 26th July, 1993, it was reported that since the project would cause pollution, the environmentalists have been opposing this project. These reports have caused considerable concern and anguish in the minds of the local villagers. Now you have published a notice...and called upon interested person to file their objections, if any, to the project... I request you furnish me information about the above project. Please give information about [the] population from the village (to be shifted), lands required for the project, possible pollution...from the project, various advantages and disadvantages to the local people from the project, and the exact area over which the project would be located. These details would enable the local villagers to form their opinion about the project and they can decide whether the project should be allowed or not.[79]

Several of the letters detailed objections to the methods of land acquisition and the potential environmental impact of the project. These issues are discussed below.

Land Acquisition

Land acquisition for the project was particularly controversial because land was surveyed and appropriated for the project without notifying or compensating individuals whose land had been seized. Villagers raised the issue with the company as soon as land was acquired for the project. Apparently, engineers began to survey land for acquisition without telling the owners of their intent. This letter, written by Ashish Suresh Damanaskar, a local farmer, illustrates the process:

> I am a resident of Anjanvel village and have come to know of the Dabhol Power Project, the biggest in Asia... I understand that my land too will be needed for this project. Some people have surveyed the land

---

[79] Letter from Yashwant Bait, secretary of the Borbatlewadi-Katalwadi Mandal, to the chief engineer of the Dabhol Power Corporation, September 22, 1993. Letter on file at Human Rights Watch.

already. But I have not fully understood the details of this project. The others in the village are also equally as ignorant of this project.

I request you to provide me with more information of this project at the above address. It is regrettable that people to be affected by this project are in the dark. I wish that, along with the nation, my village too stands to benefit from this project. Once again, I request you to provide me with this information.[80]

According to other letters received by the company, engineers began surveying and acquiring land without discussing issues such as compensation or the amount of land with local residents and landowners. The following excerpt is from a letter written by Abdul Mustan, a village leader, on behalf of the Chogale family:

We wish to inform you that the proposed Dabhol Power Corporation project is to be set up on the coast of the Vasisthi river in Guhagar Taluka and 400 acres of land is going to be acquired for this project. The land has been surveyed. We own lands comprised in four survey numbers out of the land surveyed for the project. We have planted mango trees and other fruit bearing trees in this land. We do not intend to give our lands for the project on any terms. We strongly oppose the project if our lands are going to be acquired.[81]

The DPC's version of the issues played down residents' concerns. For example, the March 1997 issue of the company publication, *Dabhol Samvad: The Monthly Bulletin of the Dabhol Power Company,* looked back blithely:

Early on, some people had started spreading stories how mango and cashew trees will be affected because of the project. Today we have mango and cashew trees growing right around the project site.[82]

---

[80] Letter from Ashish Suresh Damanaskar to the Dabhol Power Corporation, September 23, 1993. Letter on file at Human Rights Watch.

[81] Letter to the Dabhol Power Corporation from Abdul Ajij Alli Mustan, October 20, 1993. Letter on file.

[82] *Dabhol Samvad: The Monthly Bulletin of the Dabhol Power Company*, Vol. 1, No. 2, March 1997, p. 1.

In terms of providing information to local communities, the government was no better than the company. In an interview that appeared in *Dabhol Samvad*, the chief executive officer of the Maharashtra Industrial Development Corporation, A. Ramakrishnan, explained that there would be no displacement of villagers, but that agricultural land would be acquired. His explanation was opaque, however:

> There will be no physical displacement of people... We are going to take land which is under farming. Land which is under intense farming or used for agricultural activity will not be acquired. Hence, no one will be directly affected.[83]

In 1997, the company also offered jobs to families affected by the project from 1993 through 1997.[84] Villagers found this offer to be inadequate, given that they would lose their primary source of livelihood—agriculture—from land acquisition. Mahadev Satley, employed as an office worker in Bombay, is from Nagdewadi village. He was arrested during a demonstration against the company on May 15, 1997 when police detained and beat demonstrators. Satley explained why a job was less desirable than land:

> We are opposed to the project because people [here] are totally integrated with the ecosystem. If there is a family of seven people who work the land, when a project like this comes, only one will be employed, and there is no guarantee of the length of employment.[85]

Environmental Degradation

Coupled with land acquisition, concern over environmental impact fostered opposition to the project and dominated correspondence with the company. The three primary areas of concern were: the pollution of fresh water, diversion of fresh water to the project site, and the potential contamination of salt water which would adversely affect fishing communities. Indeed, degradation of fresh water, used for consumption and irrigation, has been a serious problem for villages surrounding the project since 1994 when construction first began. The effect, if any, on sea water will not be known until the project goes on-line in March 1999.

---

[83] Ibid, pp. 3-4.
[84] Ibid.
[85] Human Rights Watch interview with Mahadev Satley, Bombay, February 6, 1998.

Fresh water

According to Enron's estimates, the project will circulate about 8,338 liters of fresh water per minute.[86] Consequently, local water supplies were diverted to the project, at the expense of villagers. Professor Pawar explained:

> [W]here there is water, there is prosperity. Farmers desperately need water. Had they [the government] provided water, the entire region would have become prosperous. People are angry about this. For thirty years, people have demanded water without any success... Now people are not amused to see water shipped to Enron.[87]

The problem of fresh water diversion became so severe in 1996-1997 that the company agreed to provide villagers with water, brought in tankers. Later the DPC dug wells in villages, attempting to offset the water shortages. The water supply scheme was announced in *Dabhol Samvad*:

> The summer of 1996 reflected the need for urgent provision of drinking water to the nodal villages around the project. Our community development team studied the issue and discussed with various people how we can combine to supplying drinking water to at least some of our neighbors.[88]

The company did not make a firm commitment to restore the water supply to its original levels but only agreed to supply the amount that wells and tankers could bring to affected villages. The company noted that the "success of the program will also depend on the extent and level of ground water in the area."[89] The results are not promising. S.D. Khare, a local leader of opposition to the Dabhol Power project who provides legal aid to villagers arrested for their participation in protests against the project, noted that before the project, the villages had 300,000 liters of water daily. Enron's programs only provide 40,000 liters of water a day and have

---

[86] Enron Power Development Corporation, *Project Report for the Dabhol Power Project*, Submitted to the Central Electricity Authority, April 1993, p. 5. Report on file at Human Rights Watch.

[87] Human Rights Watch interview with Sadanand Pawar.

[88] *Dabhol Samvad...*, p. 5.

[89] Ibid.

been unable to fulfill the request to provide 100,000 liters of water a day.[90] Consequently, even with the company providing water, the villagers are notably worse-off than they were before 1994.

In the village of Veldur, this problem was compounded by sewage contamination of potable water, as a result of the project. In 1995, the company built latrines for construction workers at the site. The waste was indiscriminately discharged into the local water supply. When this was brought to the attention of the company, DPC agreed to supply water to Veldur and other villages. Residents reported that the amount of water supplied was far below the needs of villagers and did not solve the problem of adequate water supplies.[91] The day-to-day realities were described to us by one person studying the issue:

> Villagers used to have drinking water twenty-four hours a day. Since the Enron project started, they only have one hour of water a day. In contrast, Enron has its own pipeline and wastes water regularly. For two months in June and July [1997], there was no drinking water. Villagers would have to go to the river, but now, untreated sewage is dumped into the river and the water is unpotable.[92]

Given the detrimental impact on villagers, further diversion of water to DPC could only lead to increased tensions. For example, on February 7, 1997, Enron diverted water from the Aareygaon dam at the Modkagar reservoir, which it had not tapped before. Villagers who received their water from the reservoir were forced to live with significantly diminished water supplies. This would lead to protests and mass arrests of demonstrators (see Section V below).[93]

---

[90] S.D. Khare, "Report on Violations of Human Rights by Enron," Guhagar village, July 1997, p. 22. Khare documented the environmental, social, and economic problems that the project created. He also documented human rights violations by police against opponents of the project. These were detailed in this report.

[91] Ibid, pp. 22-23.

[92] Human Rights Watch interview with R. Priya, Bombay, February 4, 1998. Priya is a graduate student at Georgia Tech University in the United States, studying the effect of the project on the environment and local communities.

[93] Mangesh Chavan, "Anti-Enron Agitations," *Indranet Journal* (Bombay), September 1997, pp. 2-3.

Contamination of salt water

The other water-based issue of concern, particularly to fishing villages, is the effect of hot-water discharge into bodies of water where fishing takes place once the project goes on-line in 1999. The water is first used to cool the Dabhol Power plant. According to the minutes of a meeting between Enron and government officials on March 13, 1993, "Bobby Farris, General Manager, Enron indicated that sea water cooling is required, water requirement for the plant will be around 2,500 gallons per minute (13.5 million liters per day)...."[94]

Once the water is circulated through the plant, it is to be discharged back into the sea at a higher temperature. The water, which may also contain toxic effluents, can be expected to raise the ambient temperature of the water and may cause pollution which will kill fish and prawns, thereby destroying the fisherpeoples' means of subsistence. These concerns were raised in 1993, when individuals sent letters to the company during the two-month notification period. This is an excerpt from a letter written by a local organization concerned about the project's impact on communities:

> It is learnt from the meeting held by the collector of Ratnagiri on October 8, 1993 that the sea water will be taken in through the pipeline and released outside. The water which will be released will be five degrees Celsius higher. If this water is released in the sea, it will affect fishing. About 2,000 families of fisherfolk are living off fishing done near the seashore. If the released water affects the fish in the sea, the families of the fisherfolk may suffer a lot. The water to be released out, should be left in the deep sea, after releasing its temperature. Care should be taken that the pipeline won't come in the way of fishing.[95]

Vithal Padyal, a resident of Veldur village, has two sons who work as laborers for DPC. His sons were arrested during a police raid on Veldur on June 3, 1997 (see Section V below). Padyal explained the environmental problems the project creates and its consequent impact on the community's means of sustenance:

---

[94] Minutes of the meeting between government officers and Enron held on March 12, 1993 at MSEB's Head Office to discuss about the Dabhol Power Project, transcribed March 26, 1993, p. 4. Minutes of meeting on file at Human Rights Watch.

[95] Letter from the Vidhut Prakalp Dakshata Committee, Veldur to the chief engineer, Dabhol Power Corporation, October 11, 1993. Letter on file at Human Rights Watch.

> The [Dabhol Power] project has benefits and losses. As and when they start discharging hot water into the sea, the whole community will be at a loss. Even today, drinking water tastes different due to contaminants and sewage. The only benefit of the project is that, at the moment, it generates some income opportunity for our sons. But opposition to the project is justified. So far all our earlier generations sustained themselves on the sea. When the fisheries are destroyed by hot water discharge, what are the next generations going to do for their livelihood?[96]

Warnings of Protests

The most striking aspect of the letters sent to the company under the rules of the Electricity (Supply) Act, 1948 was that people notified the company that a failure to disclose information on environmental impact and land acquisition could lead to demonstrations against the project. For example, Nishikant Joshi, a director of M.I.D.C., a former member of the Maharashtra state legislative assembly, and the publisher of the *Daily Sagar,* a local newspaper, sent a letter to DPC detailing steps the company should take to ensure the success of the project. Excerpts of the letter state:

> I have received a small folder on [the] Dabhol Power Project which was circulated by the Chief Minister's Office. This folder gives some technical information but does not answer various questions and doubts arising in the mind of the common man. As the folder is in the English language, it is of no use to the common man. I sincerely wish that a small attractive folder giving information on various aspects of the project will be very effective and helpful to sort out various probable problems in the area. The information should cover the following aspects:—
>
> 1. Approx. requirement of land
> 2. Approx. rate [of compensation]
> 3. Employment potentiality
> 4. Procurement of raw material
> 5. Pollution problems

---

[96] Human Rights Watch interview with Vithal Padyal, Veldur village, February 14, 1998.

Background to the Protests: Ratnagiri District

    6. Development activities and public amenities to be provided
    7. Ancillary units

The Sterlite Project in Ratnagiri had to face very serious challenges from the local people, for the Company did not give any information about the project and thousands of people started opposing the unit due to fear of pollution. I think your organization should take all the care which will pave the way for [a] smooth start.[97]

P.K. Dali, the director of a local NGO, sent a similar letter to the company because of dissatisfaction over land acquisition. Dali reported that unless the company addressed this issue, protests were sure to ensue:

In Anjanvel, Veldur, and Ranavi villages, you have started survey work in which you have been resorting to activities like cutting trees, damaging stone-wall compounds, making roads, etc. without prior permission of the concerned land-holders. The land-holders have been put to loss to the extent of thousands of rupees. You are requested to stop this encroachment at once or else the local people will have to start an agitation. You are requested to take immediate cognizance of this letter.[98]

One letter, written on October 20, 1993 by Gajanan Dixit, a schoolteacher in Ratnagiri district, details the reasons for opposition to the project. Dixit was later arrested in 1997 for his participation in demonstrations against the project. He was one of the men arrested on January 29, 1997 in order to prevent him from participating in a protest on January 30 (see Section V below). His letter to DPC states:

If my lands are to be acquired for [the] Dabhol Power Project, I have objection to the project... I have been trying for the last one month to find out whether the DPC proposes to acquire my lands or not... You have issued a notice inviting objections to the project but the land-

---

[97] Letter from Nishikant Joshi to the chief engineer of the Dabhol Power Corporation, September 25, 1993. M.I.D.C.'s letter on file at Human Rights Watch.

[98] Letter from P.K. Dali to the chief engineer of the Dabhol Power Corporation, October 25, 1993. Letter on file at Human Rights Watch.

holders in the area are not being told whether their lands are being acquired or not. It is necessary to know these details...

The project is bound to bring in pollution and you are bound to say that there would not be any pollution. Please provide for my training in your Veldur laboratory. I hold a M.S. [Master of Science] degree in Chemistry and I can monitor the effects of pollution on the environment and if the report of a local person is placed before the people, they are more likely to believe it. People would then have more faith in you.[99]

Organization of Opposition to the Project

In response to villagers' growing concern, local nongovernmental organizations were formed to protest the Dabhol Power project, including the Enron Virodhi Sangharsh Samiti (Organization to Oppose Enron), and the Guhagar Taluka Enron Vaa Salgana Prakalp Virodhi Sangharsh Samiti (Guhagar District People's Forum for Opposing Enron and Other Related Projects). These organizations comprise social activists, lawyers, villagers affected by the project, local political figures and other individuals.

In addition, activists and nongovernmental organizations of various political affiliations based in other areas of India observed the developments in Ratnagiri, viewing them as part of a pattern of non-consultative environmentally dangerous "development" decisions. As local opposition to the Dabhol Power project increased, these activists and organizations expressed support for and participated in local demonstrations against the company. Among the national and regional organizations involved were the Bargi Bandh Vistapit Sangathana (Bargi Dam Displaced People's Organization), Konkan Sangharsh Samiti (Save the Konkan Organization), the Narmada Bachao Andolan (Movement to Save the Narmada River), the Samajawadi Jan Parishad (Socialist People's Conference), the Sarvodaya Vikas Manch (Organization for the Complete Development of All People), and the National Alliance for People's Movements (NAPM).

In 1996, local protests against the Dabhol Power project began in earnest. As described below in Section V, the demonstrators were met with direct repression, and those perceived as protest leaders were repeatedly harassed, both physically and through abuse of the law. In the following section we describe the legal framework under which these abuses took place.

---

[99] Letter from Gajanan Dixit to the chief engineer of the Dabhol Power Corporation, October 20, 1993. Letter on file at Human Rights Watch.

According to Katy Irani, a representative of CITU, and a participant in the district-level protests, the state government's repressive response to protests was, in part, due to a desire to build confidence with Enron following the suspension of the project. Irani told Human Rights Watch:

> Enron was initially skeptical of the [Shiv] Sena government. The civil and political rights violations that occurred under the current government happened because the [Shiv] Sena had to prove that they would safeguard Enron's interests.[100]

---

[100] Human Rights Watch interview with Katy Irani, Bombay, January 24, 1998.

IV. Legal Restrictions Used to Suppress Opposition to the Dabhol Power Project

The state government has invoked several laws to restrict peaceful expression and assembly in Ratnagiri and surrounding districts. These include provisions under the Bombay Police Act, the Code of Criminal Procedure, and the Indian Penal Code. The Bombay Police Act and the Code of Criminal Procedure have been regularly used to criminalize group demonstrations against the Dabhol Power project and to prevent individuals whom the police perceive as leaders of protests from entering the districts where opposition is active. The Indian Penal Code has been used to charge individuals known as leaders of anti-DPC protests with criminal offences as serious as attempted murder, which carries a maximum sentence of life imprisonment, even when there is little or no evidence that these individuals were involved in a crime. In several cases, these arrests have been coupled with the use of excessive force by police in the form of beatings with *lathis* (police batons or canes), fists, and sticks.

The application of these laws against peaceful opponents of the Dabhol Power project represents a systematic effort on the part of the Maharashtra government to suppress freedom of expression and peaceful assembly in violation of international standards enshrined in the International Covenant on Civil and Political Rights (ICCPR).[101] The methods used to implement the laws, in turn, violate international norms governing the conduct of law enforcement officers, most notably prohibitions against torture enshrined under the ICCPR and the United Nations Code of Conduct for Law Enforcement Officials.

---

[101] India ratified the ICCPR on April 10, 1979. The relevant articles of the ICCPR enumerating these protections are: Article 19—1. Everyone shall have the right to hold opinions without interference. 2. Everyone shall have the right to freedom of expression; this right shall include freedom to seek, receive and impart information and ideas of all kinds, regardless of frontiers, either orally, in writing or in print, in the form of art, or through any other media of his choice. 3. The exercise of the rights provided for in paragraph 2 of this article carries with it special duties and responsibilities. It may therefore be subject to certain restrictions, but these shall only be such as are provided by law and are necessary: (a) For respect of the rights or reputations of others; (b) For the protection of national security or of public order (ordre public), or of public health or morals. Article 21—The right of peaceful assembly shall be recognized. No restrictions may be placed on the exercise of this right other than those imposed in conformity with the law and which are necessary in a democratic society in the interests of national security or public safety, public order (ordre public), the protection of public health or morals or the protection of the rights and freedoms of others.

The Bombay Police Act

The most common method used by the police to restrict freedom of expression and freedom of assembly in the district has been to invoke sections 37(1) and 37(3) of the Bombay Police Act—colloquially known as "prohibitory orders" because they permit the police to prohibit various kinds of public assembly.

According to lawyers Human Rights Watch consulted in Bombay, the Bombay Police Act is intended to deter armed gangs and prevent violent riots and other clashes by armed groups, and its provisions reflect these concerns.[102] For example, among its provisions, Section 37(1) of the act prohibits the "carrying of arms, cudgels, swords, spears, bludgeons, guns, knives, sticks or lathis, or any other article, which is capable of being used for causing physical violence...the carrying of any corrosive substance or explosives...the carrying, collection and preparation of stones or other missiles or instruments or means of casting or impelling missiles" and empowers the police to "prohibit certain acts for prevention of disorder." Section 37(3) of the act allows the police to "prohibit any assembly or procession whenever and for so long as it considers such prohibition to be necessary for the preservation of the public order." However, Section 37(3) cannot be imposed indefinitely and must be renewed at fifteen-day intervals.[103]

The act also contains provisions that do not allude to violence and can be used to restrict peaceful expression and assembly. Such prohibitions include "public utterance of cries, singing of songs, playing of music" and the "delivery of

---

[102] Human Rights Watch interviews with Colin Gonzalves, Bombay, January 24, 1998 and Sunip Sen, Bombay, February 4, 1998. Gonzalves is a Bombay High Court lawyer who specializes in human rights.

[103] Section 37(1) prohibits: (a) the carrying of arms, cudgels, swords, spears, bludgeons, guns, knives, sticks or lathis, or any other article, which is capable of being used for causing physical violence, (b) the carrying of any corrosive substance or explosives, (c) the carrying, collection and preparation of stones or other missiles or instruments or means of casting or impelling missiles, (d) the exhibition of persons or corpses of figures or effigies thereof, (e) public utterance of cries, singing of songs, playing of music, (f) delivery of harangues, the use of gestures or mimetic representations, and the preparation, exhibition or dissemination of pictures, symbols, placards or any other object or thing which may in the opinion of such authority offend against decency or morality or undermine the security of or tend to overthrow the State. Section 37(3) states: The authority empowered under subsection (1) may also be order in writing prohibit any assembly or procession whenever and for so long as it considers such prohibition to be necessary for the preservation of the public order: Provided that no such prohibition shall remain in force for more than fifteen days without the sanction of the State Government.

harangues, the use of gestures or mimetic representations, and the preparation, exhibition or dissemination of pictures, symbols, placards or any other object or thing which may in the opinion of such authority offend against decency or morality...." These provisions have been used as the justification for criminalizing demonstrations against the Dabhol Power project.

The protests against the project were generally peaceful, however. This was confirmed to Human Rights Watch by the officer-in-charge of the Guhagar police, Assistant Sub-Inspector P.G. Satoshe, the commanding officer over the Maharashtra Police and State Reserve Police Force who deal with the protesters.[104] According to Satoshe:

> During the agitations, we asked the people to cooperate with the police... There have only been two violent agitations, on January 30 and June 2, [1997] the rest were peaceful.[105]

The broad loophole of the Bombay Police Act permits its application to those who gather solely to exercise their rights to free expression or assembly. Individuals charged with violating "prohibitory orders" (Section 37) are arrested, and under Section 135 of the act, which authorizes arrest and punishment for violations of Section 37, they are subject to a penalty of up to one year's imprisonment. Since 1994, sections 37 and 135 have been used to criminalize peaceful demonstrations against the Dabhol Power project. In this context, individuals arrested under Section 37 are released on personal bonds, but their cases remain unresolved because of delays in the judicial process.

The Center for Holistic Studies, a Bombay-based nongovernmental organization, reported that 233 unarmed protesters were arrested under Section 37 and Section 135 on November 8, 1994. Among the protesters were two leaders of the demonstrations, Dr. Vinay Natu, a local BJP member of the legislative

---

[104] Human Rights Watch interview with Assistant Sub-Inspector, P.G. Satoshe, Guhagar police station, February 15, 1998. On January 30, 1997, demonstrations at the Guhagar police station was met with police violence after protesters and police began to throw stones at each other and broke a water pipe leading to the project. On June 2, laborers for DPC and villagers in Veldur engaged in shouting matches and scuffles. Police dispersed the opposing parties by firing one round of ammunition into the air. As to police conduct, Satoshe's comment is implies negotiations but in this sense is misleading. For example, police launched a brutal retaliatory raid against residents of Veldur on June 3 described below in Section V.

[105] Human Rights Watch interview with Assistant Sub-Inspector, P.G. Satoshe.

assembly and president of an organization to oppose DPC (the Guhagar-Chiplun-Dapoli Parisar Bachav Sangharsh Samiti), and Vithal "Baba" Bhalekar, a recognized leader of fisherpeople in Veldur village who are opposed to the project. They were released the same day on personal bonds.[106] It is worth noting that the portion of Section 37 used to justify the arrest was subsection (1) referring to the carrying of arms or explosives or missiles, although the protest was peaceful.

Two days later, on November 10, 1994, police arrested 105 protesters under Section 37 for staging a peaceful demonstration in protest of land acquisition by the state on behalf of DPC and the impact of the project on fisherpeople. They were released on personal bonds the same day.[107]

Responding immediately to the arrests and expressing their support for the protesters' grievances, another 650 villagers, led by the former *sarpnach* (village leader) of Anjanvel village, Mahmood Mastan, peacefully demonstrated later on November 10 at the DPC site and all of the 650 protesters were arrested under Section 37 on the same day. The demonstrators were released on personal bonds the same day.[108]

Following these arrests, the district collector (the most senior law enforcement official at the district level) imposed prohibitory orders on Guhagar Taluka (sub-district), Ratnagiri district, under Section 37 of the Bombay Police Act from November 11 to November 23, 1994.[109]

This pattern would resume in 1997. After the CITU case against the company and the Maharashtra state government was dismissed, the Ratnagiri police imposed Section 37 on Ratnagiri district at fifteen-day intervals beginning on January 6, 1997. The prohibition was extended regularly and was still in force as of October 1998. When Human Rights Watch visited the district in February 1998, police were still regularly arresting protesters under the act.

The Code of Criminal Procedure

Section 144 of the Code of Criminal Procedure allows the district magistrate or district collector to "direct any person to abstain" from a district for up to sixty days, if the official "considers that such direction is likely to prevent, or tends to prevent obstruction, annoyance or injury to any person lawfully employed, or danger to human life, health or safety, or a disturbance of the public tranquility, or

---

[106] Winin Pereira, Subhash Sule, and Abhay Mehta, "Enron Update," *Indranet Journal* (Bombay), Vol. 3, No. 5-6, 1994, pp. 16-17.
[107] Ibid.
[108] Ibid.
[109] Ibid.

a riot, or an affray." [110] Section 151 of the Code of Criminal Procedure allows the police to arrest any person for a period of up to twenty-four hours, without a warrant, if they know that a crime is about to be committed and that there is no other way to prevent the crime.[111]

These laws, like Section 37 of the Bombay Police Act, are also colloquially referred to as "prohibitory orders" or "externment orders", but their implementation is different from sections 37 and 135 of the Bombay Police Act. While the Bombay Police Act contains similar provisions, the provisions in the Code of Criminal Procedure have been used to prevent individuals perceived as leaders of protests from participating in demonstrations either by placing them under preventative detention or by prohibiting their entry into the districts where demonstrations took place. When the Code of Criminal Procedure is invoked against leaders who are not from the districts, the relevant restrictions are referred to as prohibitory orders. When local villagers are prohibited from participating in demonstrations, they are referred to as externment orders. Human Rights Watch believes that the intent and application of the Code of Criminal Procedure, in this context, is to prevent leaders of the opposition to the Dabhol Power project from exercising their rights of freedom of expression and assembly.

The Indian Penal Code

An aspect of police behavior that illustrates a pervasive police bias against villagers opposed to the Dabhol Power project is the misuse of the Indian Penal Code to harass individuals opposed to the DPC project by falsely charging these individuals with offenses such as arson, criminal intimidation, or attempted murder.

Individuals charged under the Indian Penal Code can face the possibility of lengthy prison sentences. Attempted murder, for example, carries a maximum sentence of life imprisonment. In addition to prison sentences, arrests carry other hardships including hefty fines, high legal costs, and lengthy judicial proceedings.

---

[110] Section 144(1) of the Code of Criminal Procedure. For a detailed analysis of this provision, see: "The Code of Criminal Procedure," Justice M. Hidayatullah and S.P. Sathe, eds., (Nagpur: Wadhwa & Company, 1992), pp. 148-153.

[111] Section 151 of the Code of Criminal Procedure states: " (1) A police officer knowing of a design to commit any cognizable offence may arrest, without orders from the Magistrate and without a warrant, the person so designing, if it appears to such officer that the commission of the offence cannot be otherwise prevented. (2) No person arrested under sub-section (1) shall be detained for a period exceeding twenty-four hours from the time of his arrest unless his further detention is required or authorised under any other provisions of this Code or of any other law for the time being in force."

For a poor villager in a rural area, the costs and time involved in resolving a case can be extremely taxing.

V. Ratnagiri: Violations of Human Rights 1997

Beginning in 1994, when construction of the Dabhol Power project began in Ratnagiri, local farmers, shop-keepers, fisherpeople, politicians, and other residents of the district staged protests against it. Protests ceased in 1995 through the end of 1996, because construction at the site was suspended due to the cancellation of the project by the Shiv Sena-BJP government and during consideration of the CITU case.

Less than a month after the dismissal of the CITU case in December 1996, demonstrations against the DPC project resumed in Ratnagiri district. With the exception of one incident of stone-throwing and one incident in which a water pipeline was damaged, these protests were peaceful and at no time did opponents of the project advocate violence. The police response was abusive, however. For example, Dr. S.B. Bhale, who since January 1997 has worked at the Guhagar rural government hospital—the hospital closest to the Dabhol Power project—commented on police brutality during demonstrations:

> If the police actually bring people for treatment, they may bring them to the government hospital. I have seen at least ten to fifteen people over the last year who were brought by the police after demonstrations. All of these people had injuries consistent with beatings by lathis: contusions, abrasions, cuts. Two people had fractures on their arms and hands because of beatings with lathis. When people are brought by police, the doctors do not take medical histories, they just treat their wounds. The police will take their information at the station and tell the hospital people to "just treat them."[112]

The abuses took place in the context of a state of emergency that had been imposed for DPC's benefit, and those responsible were state agents acting at the company's request with additional surveillance provided by DPC.

After a brutal police raid on June 3, 1997 (see below), demonstrations became less frequent, because villagers feared the repressive tactics of police and many were facing charges still under adjudication. However, local opposition to the project remained strong. Ataman More, a local leader of the opposition to the project, told Human Rights Watch in early 1998, "[P]eople still oppose the project

---

[112] Human Rights Watch interview with Dr. S.B. Bhale, Guhagar village, February 15, 1998.

and protests could intensify except for the police atrocities and harassment."[113] Prohibitory orders were still being renewed at fifteen-day intervals, and criminal proceedings against opponents of the Dabhol Power project continued to be adjudicated.[114]

This report focuses on a series of thirty demonstrations that took place—at the height of opposition to the Dabhol Power project—between January 13 and June 1997 in Guhagar and Chiplun, population centers in Ratnagiri district.

Arrests of Protesters

According to three Indian human rights organizations—the Center for Holistic Studies, the All India Peoples' Resistance Forum (AIPRF), and the Committee to Protect Democratic Rights (CPDR)—120 protesters were arrested between January 13 and January 18, 1997. The protesters came from the villages of Anjanvel, Ranavi, and Veldur and had demonstrated at the DPC site in groups of twenty-five. They were released on personal bonds.

Three simultaneous demonstrations occurred on January 30, 1997: one in front of the Guhagar police station, a second in front of the home of a local Member of the Legislative Assembly (MLA), and a third on the Guhagar-Chiplun road. At two of these demonstrations became disruptive; at one, stones were thrown by some protesters, and at the other, protesters inadvertently damaged police barricade while surging toward it.

- The protest at the Guhagar police station, involving more than 1,800 people, was dispersed by police after a barricade was broken. Police arrested approximately 450 of the participants and charged them with violating prohibitory orders and unlawful assembly under Section 37 of the Bombay Police Act.[115]

- In front of the MLA's home, police did not arrest the demonstrators. Surendra Thatte, a recognized community leader and a candidate for the lower house of Parliament, participated in this rally. According to Thatte, police concentrated their attention on the third demonstration:

---

[113] Human Rights Watch interview with Ataman More, Veldur village, February 14, 1998.

[114] Indian People's Tribunal for Human Rights, Submission on Enron in India, April 17, 1998, p. 4.

[115] The protesters were charged under sections 37(1), 37(3), and 135 of the Bombay Police Act.

> We were not arrested even though we staged a *road roko* [road block] with 400 people. But the people, almost 2,000 at the company gates, were arrested. They were singled out for teargassing and a lathicharge.[116]

- About 1,500-2,000 protesters had marched from Guhagar village to the site of the Dabhol Power project. The protests largely consisted of shouting slogans and chants in front of the company gates. The police response was out of all proportion: protesters were beaten during a lathicharge, teargassed, and then arrested. Ms. Snehal Vaidya, head of the village council at Anjanvel, described the protest to an AIPRF fact-finding team led by retired Bombay High Court Justice S.M. Daud:

> At 9:30 in the morning as we started out in a *morcha* [protest march], shouting slogans against Enron, MNC's [multinational corporations], and the Alliance Government, the police tried to surround us and obstruct our progress. However, due to our massive numbers they were unsuccessful and we reached the site of the main demonstrations. Here, however, there was a huge police force deployed and even as we were peacefully shouting slogans, they began pushing and obstructing us... Suddenly, without warning, began a brutal lathicharge. Many of the constables were armed with freshly cut branches of trees, others with lathis, with which they indiscriminately beat up all those who had gathered.[117]

Ataman More, a local leader of protests from the fishing village of Veldur, described the actions of police when we interviewed him on February 14, 1998:

> We were stopped at the [DPC] site. We told the police that we were peaceful demonstrators and we would go to a predetermined,

---

[116] Human Rights Watch interview with Surendra Thatte, Guhagar, February 14, 1998. "Lathicharge" refers to a group of police forcibly dispersing a crowd by storming the crowd while beating them with police batons.

[117] S.M. Daud, A. Gajbhiye, V. Karkhelikar, and Stephen Rego, "In the Service of a Multinational: How the Indian State Deals with Popular Resistance to Enron," a fact-finding mission for the All India Peoples' Resistance Forum (AIPRF), April 1997, Bombay, p. 13.

preannounced site to hold our rally. If anything happens, the leaders will take responsibility for them. Despite our request, the police fired teargas shells and lathi-charged us at around 11:00 a.m. They were shooting teargas right into the crowd. Then the men and women police started beating people with lathis. I was hit with a lathi on my left thigh. People scattered and were running in all directions with the police chasing them. The ones caught by the police were dragged into police vans.[118]

Snehal Vaidya also noted that protesters were beaten and then held within the gates of the Dabhol Power Corporation by police. She told the AIPRF fact-finding team:

A number of aged men and women were not spared, including Arkatte, Mastan, Bangi (in their seventies) and eighty-three year old Chiplunkar. Totally seventeen women and five men were severely beaten. Ms. Parvati Saitavadekar, Bangi and the severely paralyzed Gurav, who were injured were pushed into the company compound and left without medical treatment for hours... [W]e were forcibly pushed into the police van, and minutes later, the police began firing tear-gas shells.[119]

According to the AIPRF fact-finding team, approximately forty canisters of teargas were fired and several rounds of ammunition were shot in the air. The police reportedly threw stones at fleeing protesters. In total, police arrested 679 people and charged them under Section 37 and Section 135 of the Bombay Police Act. The protesters were presented before the magistrate at Chiplun on January 30 and 31 and were released on personal bonds. Many of the cases, however, were still pending in October 1998.

On February 7, 1997, the DPC diverted water from the Aareygaon dam at the Modkagar reservoir. Villagers who received their water from the reservoir were forced to live with significantly diminished water supplies. In protest, approximately one hundred villagers, led by retired Bombay High Court Justice B.G. Kolse-Patil, staged a sit-in that blocked the pumps transporting water to the

---

[118] Human Rights Watch interview with Ataman More, Veldur village, February 14, 1998.

[119] "In the Service of a Multinational...", p. 13.

Dabhol Power project. During the demonstration, a water pipe was broken by protesters.[120]

Twelve days later, on February 19, a pump operator at the dam restored the water supply to Enron, but villagers learned about the diversion of water and tried to stop him by blocking access to the pump. The operator filed a complaint with the police. Seven villagers were arrested on February 27 and one was arrested on March 15 for violating prohibitory orders under Section 37 and unlawful assembly under the Indian Penal Code.[121] They were released on 1,000 rupees bail the day of their arrest.

In the village of Pawarsakhari, approximately 250 protesters held a road roko (road block protest) on February 21 to prevent two state cabinet ministers, Narayan Rane and Ravindra Rane, from going through the village because they supported the project. In response, a battalion of the State Reserve Police lathi-charged the protesters and arrested ninety-six people. They were charged with violating prohibitory orders under Section 37 and unlawful assembly under the Indian Penal Code.[122]

On April 28, 1997, approximately 150 members of the Samajwadi Jan Parishad (Socialist Peoples' Conference) from four states—Bihar, Orissa, Uttar Pradesh, and West Bengal—were arrested for protesting in front of the Dabhol Power project gates. They were charged with violating prohibitory orders under Section 37 and sentenced to nine days' imprisonment.[123]

Two days later, fifty people were arrested for protesting in front of the site and for violating prohibitory orders under Section 37. They were sentenced to thirteen days' imprisonment by the judicial magistrate at Chiplun.[124]

On May 4 and May 6, 1997, two peaceful demonstrations took place at the gates of the Dabhol Power project. Eleven people were arrested on May 4 and fifty individuals on May 6. All were arrested for violating prohibitory orders under Section 37 and were sentenced to fifteen days' imprisonment.[125]

---

[120] "Anti-Enron Agitations...," pp. 2-3.

[121] The protesters were charged under sections 37(1), 37(3), and 135 of the Bombay Police Act and Section 143 of the Indian Penal Code.

[122] The protesters were charged under sections 37(1), 37(3), and 135 of the Bombay Police Act and Section 143 of the Indian Penal Code.

[123] "Anti-Enron Agitations...," pp. 3-4.

[124] Ibid.

[125] Ibid., p. 4.

On May 15, 1997, Medha Patkar and approximately 178 other villagers were arrested for violating prohibitory orders by participating in a sit-in near the gates of the Dabhol Power project.[126] Some of the demonstrators were beaten by police near the company's gates. Following a judicial hearing, all were released the next day.[127]

Mahadev Satley, who is employed as an office assistant in Bombay but grew up in the village of Nagewadi in Ratnagiri district, participated in the May 15 demonstration. He told Human Rights Watch that once the protesters reached the plant gate, approximately 400 protesters put up banners, shouted slogans and stopped vehicles from entering the project site. The protest was completely peaceful from 8:00 a.m. to 9:00 a.m. Initially there were approximately ten police officers and two police vans, but when they saw the size of the crowd, police asked for reinforcements and three more vans. A larger contingent of approximately fifty police officers, made up of Maharashtra Police and the State Reserve Police Force (SRP), arrived at the gate.

According to Satley, Circle Inspector Desmukh, the police officer responsible for supervising police in several districts, was present at the demonstration and told the activists that they would be arrested. Satley said that the police started "manhandling people" and that at least fifteen people were beaten with lathis. About fifty people were placed in the vans.[128]

Medha Patkar, a nationally and internationally known environmental activist who participated in this demonstration, told Human Rights Watch:

> After an hour, the police told us to go. We knew we were going to be arrested, so we held hands. They pulled me by the hair. The police molested many women, so they started yelling at the police which made the police more angry.[129]

Around 11:30 a.m., the protesters were taken in the vans to Guhagar police station. The police finished their paperwork by 2:00 p.m. The protesters were transported to Chiplun at around 5:30 pm and produced before the magistrate. Because the courts were closed for the day, they were held in custody overnight. The police wanted them to stay in the open, but they refused. Finally arrangements

---

[126] Ibid. National Alliance of Peoples' Movements press release, May 16, 1997.
[127] "Anti-Enron Agitations...," pp. 3-4.
[128] Ibid.
[129] Human Rights Watch interview with Medha Patkar, Bombay, February 20, 1998.

were made to keep them at the community hall. There were no sanitary facilities, and they received food only at 1:30 a.m.

The next morning, they were produced before the court. People tried to tell the judge about the lack of facilities in custody, the bad food, the travel which created further hardship because of the costs of transportation, and the beatings at the time of arrest, but the judge would not listen. In protest, the demonstrators refused to pay bail or fines and were prepared to stay in jail. Four days were spent in jail at Chiplun, after which the group of about fifty was transferred to Yerewada jail, 400 kilometers away in the city of Pune. On May 20 they were released. Satley told Human Rights Watch:

> There is a popular feeling that the Guhagar police act as employees of Enron and not guardians of law and order on behalf of the state. Not only the local police, but the local courts were colluding with Enron. Whatever the treatment we got from the time we were arrested was to please or appease Enron. The state, police, and courts were extremely harsh to show Enron that they were serious.[130]

A well-known politician with the Janata Dal, a major political party, Mrs. Mrinal Gore, led a road roko in Guhagar, along with thirty other protesters, on May 16, 1997. They were arrested by police and charged under Section 37 and Section 135 of the Bombay Police Act and wrongful restraint under the Indian Penal Code.[131] They were remanded to magisterial custody (kept in custody in jails near the court) and released on May 31. Two of the female protesters were minors and were illegally kept in the Kalyan jail.[132]

On May 17, more than 300 demonstrators were protesting the Dabhol Power Corporation's fencing of land around their farms. Police arrested and charged them under sections 37 and 135. Surendra Thatte, a participant in this demonstration, told Human Rights Watch:

> I was involved in the May 17 demonstration. Our crime was taking part in an assembly of more than four persons. This happened around 11:00. We were arrested around two or three in the afternoon. At about five in the evening, we arrived at Chiplun and were taken before the magistrate.

---

[130] Human Rights Watch interview with Mahadev Satley.
[131] Section 341 of the Indian Penal Code.
[132] "Anti-Enron Agitations...," p. 7.

The magistrate said that we violated prohibitory orders and remanded us to fourteen days' custody. Fifty women were sent to Kholapur. Sixteen men and fifty-four women were taken to Sangli, which is about four hours by bus. We were treated well in custody and kept away from undertrials and goondas [colloquial term for habitual criminals]. After fourteen days, we were brought to the magistrate and released.[133]

The same day, May 17, approximately 3,000 people from villages in the district gathered to demand that work be stopped at the Dabhol Power project site. Police did not arrest anyone at the gates. On June 3, however, the police filed a First Information Report charging 1,200 of those demonstrators under Section 37 of the Bombay Police Act. Their cases were still pending in October 1998.[134]

Targeting of Protest Leaders
During the 1997 protests against the Dabhol Power project, individuals identified as "leaders" of the opposition have been detained through the use of preventative detention laws and targeted externment orders that have restricted their movement and prohibited their entry into areas where opposition to the project was most active. The logic of these measures has been to weaken resistance by forcing villagers to participate without leadership and to demoralize those most vocal in their opposition to the project.

Sadanand Pawar, an economics professor who is from Pawarsakari village in Ratnagiri district, and a recognized leader of the protests against the DPC project, told Human Rights Watch:

> In a democracy, you have a right for a civilized demonstration, [but] this does not exist at all. Meaningful agitation cannot be organized or sustained because the police, backed by the government, victimize the people... Section 144 [of the Code of Criminal Procedure] is always there: if you hold meetings, they can frame you. Now the police are bold, they will charge you with all sorts of things... It works like this. First you will get a notice that you are an agitator, spreading false information to the people, and inspiring people to riot and destroy things. And if anything happens, you will be held responsible.[135]

---

[133] Human Rights Watch interview with Surendra Thatte.
[134] Human Rights Watch interview with Mangesh Chavan, Bombay, February 4, 1998.
[135] Human Rights Watch interview with Sadanand Pawar.

Medha Patkar and B.G. Kolse-Patil: March 1997

An excerpt from an order issued under Section 144 of the Code of Criminal Procedure on March 1, 1997, by T. Chandrasekhar, the district magistrate of Ratnagiri, the highest-ranking law enforcement officer at the district level, illustrates the intent of these orders. In this case, the prohibitory order was issued against environmentalist Medha Patkar and retired Bombay High Court Judge B.G. Kolse-Patil, two recognized leaders of demonstrations. The order states:

ORDER

Sub: Prohibitory orders issued u/s 144 of Cr.P.C.

> Whereas it has been brought to my notice that in Guhagar Taluka, Shri B.G. Kolse Patil and Smt. Medha Patkar, leaders of the Anti-Enron Agitation Group have been conducting meetings of the villagers in the Enron Power Project affected villages as well as in the surrounding villages of the Enron Project in Guhagar Taluka. It has also been brought to my notice by the Superintendent of Police, Ratnagiri, that these persons are instigating the villagers against the Dabhol Power Company (Enron Power Project) and proposed Land Acquisition by the M.I.D.C. and indulging in Rasta Roko, Morchas by violating prohibitory orders in violation of the provisions of section 37(1)(3) of the Bombay Police Act, 1951 and creating a law and order problem in Guhagar Taluka. It is apprehended that the activities of Shri B.G. Kolse Patil and Smt. Medha Patkar may cause a breach of peace and law and order problem during the ensuing Zilla Parishad Panchayat Samities Elections which are to be held on 2nd March 97. It is therefore necessary to prevent Shri Kolse Patil and Smt. Medha Patkar from entering into Ratnagiri District.[136]

The intent of the order was clear: to prohibit leading opponents of the Dabhol Power project from exercising their right to freely express their views in order to prevent opposition to the project from becoming an election issue.

---

[136] Prohibitory order issued against Medha Patkar and B.G. Kolse-Patil by T. Chandrasekhar, District Magistrate of Ratnagiri, March 1, 1997.

Medha Patkar: May 1997

Another incident involved Patkar and some of her colleagues from the National Alliance of Peoples' Movements (NAPM), and took place in the town of Mahad, near the Dabhol Power project. Under the pretense of preventing damage to property and loss of life, police served Patkar with prohibitory orders under Section 144 on May 29, 1997 and then surveilled, arrested, beat, and detained the activists—on the eve of her departing for Raigad and Ratnagiri districts with plans to lead a series of protests against the DPC project and other industrial projects. The incident merits detailed treatment. Due to its being subsequently investigated by the Indian government's National Human Rights Commission, it is unusually well documented and provides a close look at the process driving the issuance of prohibitory and externment orders.

The National Human Rights Commission determined that the order against Patkar under Section 144 of the Code of Criminal Procedure was "unjustified."[137] The behavior of the government led the commission to comment:

> The case of Ms. Medha Patkar deserves anxious attention...as some basic human rights issues are involved. In a free and democratic setup, the Fundamental Rights of individuals cannot be allowed to be infringed upon with impunity...State machinery should not be misused for ulterior aim and gains of the party in power, out to strangulate the voices of dissent.[138]

The commission determined, moreover, that the human rights violations committed by the police were due, in part, to an order given by Maharashtra Chief Minister Manohar Joshi "to deal with the situation...firmly or else the wrong signal would be conveyed to the business world."[139] At the time, Chief Minister Joshi was on a five-nation tour of Asia seeking to attract foreign investment and extoll the virtues of the business climate in Maharashtra.[140] Consequently, Joshi called More, and More, in turn, ordered the district magistrate, R.S. Rathod, to prevent Patkar

---

[137] National Human Rights Commission of India, *Enquiry Report-Alleged Human Rights Violation of Ms. Medha Patkar and Other Activists*, July 1997, p. 17. This incident, to the knowledge of Human Rights Watch, is the only case related to the DPC project that has been investigated for human rights violations by any government agency.

[138] Ibid., pp. 17-18.

[139] Ibid.

[140] V. Jayanth, "Joshi Finds The Going Tough in Singapore," *The Hindu*, May 21, 1997.

from entering the district and to stop Patkar and the other activists. The commission reported:

> Apprehending trouble, the CM [chief minister] telephonically spoke to Shri Prabhakar Raoji More, Minister of State for Home and State Minister of Industries (known as Guardian Minister for Raigad district), to handle the situation. Shri More in turn asked Shri R.S. Rathod, DM [District Magistrate], to immediately intervene and see the withdrawal of the hunger strike and frustrate the entry of Ms. Patkar to the district. The DM sprung into action and in consultation with the SP [Superintendent of Police], worked out a strategy to prevent Medha Patkar from entering the district.[141]

According to Lata P.M., deputy director of the NAPM and former director of NAPM's field office in Ratnagiri district, the prohibitory order and the police brutality occurred just after NAPM had begun a "development tour" of the region on May 28.[142] The purpose of the tour was to educate local communities about the environmental and social impacts of the Dabhol Power project and other large industrial projects in the area and to hold peaceful demonstrations against these projects.[143] Lata detailed the basis of opposition to the Dabhol Power project:

> Enron is symbolic of the impact of multinationals, globalization, and the right to information. How much displacement will there be? Will there be suitable rehabilitation? Fishworkers, farmers, mill owners, and local entrepreneurs would be impacted by the project. Already, local water is being taken by Enron. A jetty is being built and forests are being cut down. What is the environmental impact? What is the real price of power? What was the criteria of the arrangement? We worry about the impact of this and other "mega-projects." [144]

The tour began in the village of Chandva, Raigad district, where Patkar and other NAPM activists met with villagers and prepared for upcoming meetings and

---

[141] *Enquiry Report-Alleged Human Rights Violation...*, p. 3.
[142] Following this incident, Lata had to leave the Ratnagiri field office, due to her injuries and other physical ailments.
[143] Human Rights Watch interview with Lata P.M., Bombay, January 28, 1998.
[144] *Enquiry Report-Alleged Human Rights Violation...*, p. 3.

speeches. Local villagers also decided to create an organization to oppose industrial development in the region.

That evening, the superintendent of police at Raigad, V. Lokhande, received a report that a communist youth front was organizing a hunger strike at the gate of Indian Petrochemicals Limited (IPCL), another industrial project in the area, and had asked Patkar to speak there as a show of support. In addition, Lokhande received a written complaint from IPCL personnel alleging that unknown individuals might "endanger the security of the plant" and asking police to address the issue.[145]

Over the telephone, the district magistrate, R.S. Rathod, persuaded the youth front to call off its hunger strike and then apprised Minister More of the situation. Although the demonstration was canceled, Minister More, who had just spoken to Chief Minister Joshi, ordered Lokhande to restrict Patkar's entry into the district anyway and to control any "law and order" problems. Lokhande informed Rathod who, in turn, issued prohibitory orders against Patkar under Section 144 of the Code of Criminal Procedure. The prohibitory order states, in part:

> [A]nd whereas I have satisfied myself that it is necessary to take speedy steps for immediate prevention of damages to prevent human life, disturbance of public peace and tranquility, riot or affray and to maintain the law and order situation and industrial peace and the grounds brought on the record lead me to treat this as a case of emergency and accordingly to pass ex-parte order.
>
> Therefore, I do hereby u/s 144 of Cr.P.C. order and direct that you should not enter into the boundaries of Raigad District from the date of this order, i.e. 28th May, 1997 to 30th June, 1997 (both days inclusive).[146]

On the evening of May 28, the superintendent of police, V. Lokhande, ordered Special Deputy Police Officer Vijay Singh Jadhav to serve Patkar with the order and to ensure that she did not enter the district or participate in any demonstrations or other events.[147] On May 29, at approximately 7:30 a.m., Jadhav took two female police officers, one sub-inspector, and ten male officers to the

---

[145] Ibid., pp. 3-4.

[146] Prohibitory order issued to Medha Patkar by District Magistrate R.S. Rathod, May 28, 1998.

[147] *Enquiry Report-Alleged Human Rights Violation* ..., pp. 3-4.

Tolphata Highway Trijunction near the town of Mahad and waited for Patkar to approach. In addition, two police officers were sent to Chandva village "to cover the movement of Ms. Patkar and her activities covertly."[148]

Approximately fifteen minutes later, two jeeps carrying Lata and some five other activists were spotted by Sub-Inspector (SI) Magdoom, who contacted Jadhav by police radio and told him that Patkar was not in the jeeps. As the activists approached Jadhav at the trijunction, police stopped them. According to Lata:

> The police stopped the jeeps at Tolphata, a quiet place near the Mahad-Bombay highway which heads towards the Konkan highway. There were about thirteen male and two female police that attacked us, and about twenty or twenty-five more police were in accompanying police jeeps and vans.[149]

Jadhav told them that they were prohibited from holding a public meeting under Section 37 of the Bombay Police Act. When the activists protested, Jadhav informed them that they were under arrest.[150] The National Human Rights Commission determined that the arrest was illegal, since Section 37 was not operative in Mahad.[151] Lata told Human Rights Watch:

> The special deputy police officer, Mr. Jadhav, led the police. He asked people to get out of the jeeps to be checked. He told us that we had been arrested and to get into the police vans. I asked him to show us a warrant for their arrest. He refused to produce any warrant. I asked him, "Why are you arresting us since we are going to a meeting?" He said that I should not ask any questions and that he had the authority to arrest us under the Bombay Police Act.
>
> People refused to go into the van, people were standing around. One woman was sixty years old, one woman had her child with her, and three college-aged girls were there. Some were standing, some were sitting in the jeep. We told the police that we wanted to wait for Medha, because we thought she had already been arrested.[152]

---

[148] Ibid., p. 4.
[149] Human Rights Watch interview with Lata P.M.
[150] *Enquiry Report-Alleged Human Rights Violation ...*, p. 5.
[151] Ibid., p. 16.
[152] Human Rights Watch interview with Lata P.M.

Lata tried to flag down a truck in order to ask the driver to inform Patkar or their associates in Bombay of their arrest. The police intervened and told the driver of the vehicle to leave, then the police started motioning vehicles to drive on. Lata and the other activists then staged a sit-down and asked the police to provide the grounds for their arrest. In response, the two female police officers grabbed Lata by her hair and throat, smashed her head against the police van, and beat her with their lathis and fists on her head and legs.[153]

Two of the women pleaded with police to stop beating Lata, while trying to grab her away from the police. According to Lata, Sub-Inspector Vijay Kadam tried to tear the womens' clothes off and slapped Lata. While the scuffle continued, a message came over police radio that Patkar had arrived at the Mahad bus stand. The police took Lata and the others to intercept Patkar.[154]

At the bus stand, police served Patkar with the prohibitory order. At approximately 1:00 p.m., a bus destined for Bombay arrived at the bus stand. Patkar and thirty-one other activists boarded the bus with the intention of returning to Bombay. The bus driver protested their entry, citing a lack of capacity and mechanical difficulties. About an hour later, the police allowed the bus to continue towards Bombay, under a police escort.[155]

Two hours later, at approximately 4:00 p.m., the police diverted the bus to the Mangaon police station. There, police ordered passengers not affiliated with Patkar to vacate the bus "fast or they would be beaten up."[156] Once those passengers disembarked, police boarded the bus and beat the protesters. Lata, who was on the bus, told Human Rights Watch:

> When we were on the bus, two goondas [thugs] and police entered the bus and told us to get off the bus. Sub-Inspector Vijay Kadam and four female officers came. They first caught the men, then the women. One of the police officers started slapping and beating Prita, a nineteen- or twenty-year-old college student. Vijay Kadam was using the scarf of her *salwaar kameez* [a dress with a tight pant and loose top and scarf] to strangle her and was trying to tear her clothes off. Prita's sister started crying when she saw this, and then the female officers started to beat her as well. They threw Medha from the bus. I tried to save Medha, but the police grabbed me and started banging my head against

---

[153] Ibid.
[154] *Enquiry Report-Alleged Human Rights Violation...*, p. 5.
[155] Ibid., p. 6.
[156] Ibid.

the steel handrail in the bus. They started beating me on the head, which made me dizzy and disoriented. They were beating everyone on the head, and one girl was being beaten with a lathi. During this time, we kept on asking the police to produce court orders proving they had grounds for the arrest.[157]

After beating the activists, police arrested them; they were detained in the lockup at the Mangaon police station. Seven women were placed in one cell and twenty-five men in another. The police offered them food, but the activists refused. Lata told Human Rights Watch:

We were taken to jail around 3:00 [p.m.]. Even the sixty-year-old woman, Vijaya Sangvai, was literally thrown into the cell. We were kept in the cell for hours. The women were in serious pain, they were dizzy and vomiting from the beating. We were detained in a filthy ten-by-ten-foot cell. When men wanted to use the latrine, they were handcuffed like common criminals and led to the toilet.[158]

Patkar told the National Human Rights Commission that the lockups were "filthy" and that the toilets could not be used. She said that even women who required sanitary napkins were denied these requests by police. They were not allowed to see a doctor or a lawyer.[159] In fact, the National Human Rights Commission determined that although the activists' lawyer, Ms. Surekha Dalvi, made twelve phone calls to the station, police repeatedly refused to allow her to speak to her clients and then kept the phone engaged so that no one could call the station.[160]

Around 10:30 p.m., a judicial magistrate arrived at the police station, accompanied by a doctor. Patkar complained of the ill-treatment and the lack of medical and legal counsel. Of the magistrate's attitude, Lata recalled:

A doctor and magistrate were brought to the jail. When we told him how we were treated, the magistrate told us that "I don't have time to

---

[157] Human Rights Watch interview with Lata P.M.
[158] Ibid.
[159] *Enquiry Report-Alleged Human Rights Violation..*, pp. 8-9.
[160] Ibid., pp. 15-16.

listen to this." He refused to hear Medha's whole story and would not accept any oral or written statements by the arrested.[161]

The doctor concluded that "these injuries could not be possible due to assault." (Later, another doctor examined the ex-detainees in Bombay and determined that they had all "suffered from trauma, and found injury marks probably due to lathi assault, fists, etc."[162]) The magistrate ordered the protesters remanded to custody for fourteen days.

The next morning, May 30, at approximately 4:00 a.m., they were trying to sleep in the cell when Lata and some other women asked to go to the toilet. Special Deputy Police Officer Dadar told them not to go to the toilet but that they would be taken to Yerwada jail. They were led to a police bus and transported to Yerwada jail, approximately 200-250 kilometers away in Pune. Police did not allow them to use the toilet before the trip; instead they stopped on the highway at a creek and forced the people to go to the restroom there. During this brief outing, one of the arrested managed to give a note to a motorcyclist to tell NAPM in Bombay that they were in police custody.[163]

They reached Yerwada around midday. Many anti-Dabhol Power project protesters had been detained there following the protests that Patkar had been scheduled to address. They were treated well at Yerwada, and Patkar started bringing up prisoners' rights issues. Later, on May 30, lawyers and journalists came to see them. Patkar and her colleagues were released on May 31.

Patkar and others asked the chief minister to initiate a judicial inquiry into the incident, but Joshi refused and only agreed to a police enquiry. The National Human Rights Commission intervened and, among its findings, concluded that:

> Ms. Medha Patkar is a known environmentalist and has been touring the Konkan region, to create awareness amongst the people about environmental and pollution problems created by various industries/plants. She feels that multinationals entered this area with the aim to grab government land and other concessions and make quick money. This further compounded the situation. These plants have seriously endangered the ecological balance and led to ruthless exploitation of the locals who are being inhumanely evicted without

---

[161] Human Rights Watch interview with Lata P.M.
[162] *Enquiry Report-Alleged Human Rights Violation...*, pp. 8-9.
[163] Human Rights Watch interview with Lata P.M.

proper resettlement and rehabilitation. During the course of her meetings, she had also exposed various acts of corruption alleged to have been committed by the Ministers of the party in power, out to personally benefit from the deals. Her meeting evoked widespread response from the local people, especially the womenfolks.

The police, in utter disregard to the Fundamental Rights guaranteed by the Constitution, roughed up and humiliated peaceful and unarmed social workers, fighting for a benevolent cause. Even the women (young and some elderly) were not spared.[164]

The commission also found the actions of District Magistrate Rathod—who had issued the prohibitory order against Patkar—to be "prejudiced, biased, and not based on judicious discharge of his duties, as a public servant."[165] The commission was especially critical of Special Deputy Police Officer Jadhav, reporting, "His conduct was reprehensible, he took sadistic delight in committing atrocities on the unarmed and peaceful activists with the help of his subordinate police staff..." and it recommended legal action against Jadhav.[166] The commission did not, however, recommend an investigation into the role of Chief Minister Joshi or Minister More for their role in the events. As of October 1998, none of the commission's recommendations had been adopted by the state government. The commission has no power to impose punishment, and their findings remain non-binding.[167]

Externment orders: 1996-97
Local villagers have been subjected to externment under Section 144 and Section 151 of the Code of Criminal Procedure, as well. For example, Dattaram Jangli, a shop owner and community leader in the village of Borbatlewadi who was active in demonstrations against the Dabhol Power project, was served externment orders along with six other village leaders throughout 1996-1997. The following individuals were externed from Borbatlewadi: Dhondu Dasbud in December 1996; Bhikail Bane in December 1996; Janpath Bane on February 26, 1997; Raman Pardale and Rajesh Jangli on August 26, 1997. All of the orders state that the sub-

---

[164] *Enquiry Report-Alleged Human Rights Violation...*, pp. 17-18.
[165] Ibid.
[166] Ibid., p. 18.
[167] For a detailed discussion of the National Human Rights Commission, see: Human Rights Watch, *Police Abuse and Killings of Street Children in India*, (New York: Human Rights Watch, 1996), pp. 67-89.

divisional magistrate at Chiplun, under Section 144 of the Code of Criminal Procedure, seeks to extern them from Ratnagiri, Sindadur, and Raigur.

Dattaram Jangli was served an externment order in May 1997 that prohibited him from entering his village. The order does not state that he is a community leader, shop owner, and participant in protests; instead it is justified on the grounds that Jangli "lives comfortably by terrorizing the people."[168] According to Jangli, "The police know that we are leaders against Enron, so if they issue externment orders, no protests will come from this village."[169]

Arrests at Guhagar police station: January 1997

On January 29, 1997, the district collector (in charge of civil and police affairs) of Ratnagiri, P. Chandrashekar, and the deputy superintendent of police (DSP), Rajender Singh, called a meeting to discuss the planned demonstration on January 30. According to one participant in the meeting, the collector asked them, "Why are people agitating, what do you have against the company?"[170]

Sadanand Pawar, then secretary of an organization leading the demonstration, raised the issue that police were telling people not to participate in the protest and were threatening to fire on protesters the following day. After initially denying this, the collector said that if information was being spread by the police to create a "law and order" situation he would deal with it.

Between 9:30 and 10:00 p.m., local activists from Aareygaon village (about four or five activists and two villagers) came to S.D. Khare's residence because they had decided to set up the office of the protest organizing committee across the street.[171] They said that in Aareygaon, someone was spreading a rumor that a bomb blast would take place at the demonstration on January 30. Consequently, the villagers wished to lodge a complaint against the person spreading the rumor. They were under the impression that the collector and the DSP would accept the complaint because of the collector's previous assurance that he would act on any "law and order" problems.

---

[168] Human Rights Watch interview with Dattaram Jangli, Borbatlewadi village, February 15, 1998.

[169] Ibid.

[170] Human Rights Watch interview with Mangesh Chavan. Chavan is a local activist from Ratnagiri who has documented all of the arrests, beatings, and detentions due to protests against the Dabhol Power project.

[171] As noted above, Khare is known as a provider of legal assistance to arrested protesters.

About an hour later, eight or nine people went to the police station, but the Chief inspector was not there. The police told them that he was at the Sagar Lodge to check if any people from Bombay or other places who planned to participate in the demonstration had booked rooms in the hotel.

At the Sagar Lodge, the villagers told Circle Inspector Desmukh and Assistant Sub-Inspector P.G. Satoshe about the bomb rumor.[172] The officers said that they would deal with it the next day. The activists told the police that they were just doing their job by informing the police so that they would not be accused of causing problems. The two inspectors accompanied them to the Guhagar police station to lodge a formal complaint. When they entered the police station, however, Satoshe then told everyone that they were being arrested under Section 151 of the Code of Criminal Procedure.

The activists told the police that they wanted to meet with the collector or the DSP because of the previous assurances they had been given concerning "law and order" problems. Circle Inspector Desmukh told them, "Nothing doing, all your rights end here itself."[173]

One of the arrested, Adinath Kaljunkar, attempted to submit a written complaint to the police concerning the rumored bomb threat. The police refused to accept it.

Around 12:30 a.m., police transported the activists to the jail at Chiplun, approximately forty kilometers away, without allowing them to notify anyone of their arrest. At Chiplun, they were still not allowed to contact anyone and spent the night in a small, cold cell with only a thin sheet to cover them. Produced before the magistrate the next morning. they told him their story and were released on personal bonds around 6:00 p.m. According to Chavan:

> They wanted to arrest us because we were prominent citizens of Guhagar. The police knew that we were respected leaders of the community. In fact, Satoshe's daughter was being tutored by one of the people he arrested, Gajannan Dixit, a local schoolteacher.[174]

---

[172] A Circle Inspector is an inspector whose responsibilities extend to several districts.
[173] Human Rights Watch interview with Mangesh Chavan.
[174] Ibid.

Sadanand Pawar: February 1997

Sadanand Pawar was arrested under Section 151 of the Code of Criminal Procedure on two occasions. On January 29, 1997, he was among the men arrested by the Guhagar police when they went to notify the authorities about a rumored bomb threat the next day. Before he was arrested, Pawar told us, the district commissioner of police threatened to kill him if he participated in the January 30 demonstration.

In the run-up to the March 1997 *Zilla Parishad* (local government) elections, Pawar and others opposed to the project believed that the BJP had forwarded candidates who supported the Dabhol Power project in order to minimize opposition to it. Since candidates from other political parties were also supportive of the company, they felt that voting for any candidate would undermine organized opposition. Consequently, they called for a boycott of the elections.

Four days before the election, on February 28, Pawar and another activist, Mangesh Pawar, were arrested as a preventative measure under Section 151 of the Code of Criminal Procedure.[175] Police did not notify anyone that he had been arrested or later transferred to Chiplun. Pawar was kept in custody from 10:00 a.m. until about 8:30 p.m. Police took him to the magistrate at Chiplun at about 1:30 in the morning. Because it was so late, Pawar was unable to get an advocate or secure bail. Around 2:00 a.m., he was put in the lockup at Chiplun police station.

The next day, March 1, at about 4:00 p.m., some colleagues found him and obtained a lawyer. He was transferred to Ratnagiri jail and released on March 6, 1997, eight days earlier than his sentence required. The early release date, however, was conditioned on prohibiting Pawar from entering districts where there was opposition to the Dabhol Power project. The order for his release illustrates the bias police and the judiciary hold against people opposed to the Enron project. According to the order of V.G. Munshi, the sessions judge at Ratnagiri:

> The applicant/accused is protesting against the Enron project and is a leader of the anti-Enron movement. They [the police] alleged that the applicant spread false information to the public which is against Enron...

---

[175] Section 151 of the Code of Criminal Procedure states: "(1) A police officer knowing of a design to commit any cognizable offence may arrest, without orders from the Magistrate and without a warrant, the person so designing, if it appears to such officer that the commission of the offence cannot be otherwise prevented. (2) No person arrested under sub-section (1) shall be detained in custody for a period exceeding twenty-four hours from the time of his arrest unless further detention is required or authorised under any other provisions of this Code or of any other law for the time being in force."

and the applicant met voters and urged them to boycott the Z.P. [Zilla Parishad] elections. Therefore, to keep the peace in Guhagar taluka, he should be remanded for 14 days...

Taking in to consideration all the circumstances, the applicant should be released forthwith on the condition that he should not enter within the limits of Chiplun and Guhagar talukas till 31-3-97 and not to create any problem affecting law and order.[176]

While Pawar was in custody, Circle Inspector Desmukh let him know that his custody was specifically related to his participation in protests against the Dabhol Power project. Pawar recalled for Human Rights Watch :

Desmukh asked me, "How do you feel, will you continue the agitation?" They wanted to see how strong I was mentally, since I had never been in jail. I told them that I would continue agitating, it is my birthright. I was put in a terrible cell with bad smells and filth. Desmukh said, "This is what it is like in jail and if I wanted to agitate, I must face these things." I refused food and told them [the police] I was not a criminal and would begin a fast in the cell itself. After two or three hours, he assigned a constable to clean up the cell. He wouldn't put me in a clean cell because he wanted to intimidate me. He would say, "You are a professor, you earn well, why do you want these headaches?"[177]

Abuse of the Indian Penal Code

As noted above, police have abused the Indian Penal Code to falsely charge villagers opposed to the Dabhol Power project with offences ranging from unlawful assembly to attempted murder in the cases of the April 1 attack in Katalwadi village. Cases investigated by Human Rights Watch and Indian human rights organizations reveal a consistent pattern of bias by police which is exhibited when DPC contractors' property is damaged or when disputes arise between DPC contractors (who support the power project) and opponents of the Dabhol Power project. When damage occurs to the property of DPC contractors police vigorously pursue opponents of the project as primary suspects, irrespective of the facts.

---

[176] Judicial order of Sessions Judge V.G. Munshi, Ratnagiri Sessions Court, March 6, 1997.

[177] Human Rights Watch interview with Sadanand Pawar.

When a confrontation between contractors and villagers occurs, police retaliate against the villagers. When contractors threaten or attack individuals or their property, police refuse to investigate complaints or else file charges against the plaintiffs. Retaliation has included arbitrary arrests, beatings, and illegal detention of juveniles.

Regarding property damage

On December 17, 1996, at approximately 7:00 p.m., police arrested Mahadev Pandurang Solkar, Pradeep Satley, Laxman Satley, and Shankar Vane relative to the destruction of two vehicles owned by DPC contractors the day before. The police took them to Guhagar police station, approximately five kilometers away. Later, police charged the men with destruction of the vehicles and rioting.[178]

Initially, the police did not tell the men or other villagers that they were being arrested, rather that they were being taken for questioning. At the station, their names, addresses, occupations, and work addresses were recorded by the police, then they were asked whether they knew anything about the incident or who did it—which they did not. Police then informed them that they had been arrested because of the truck burnings and put them in jail.

While they were in custody, around twenty-five men and women from their hamlet came to the station and told the police that the jailed people were innocent and that no one in the hamlet knew about the incident. But the police would not listen to them. Then villagers started asking the police how they could hold a man who has just had an operation (Laxman Satley) and told them that if anything happened to him, the police would be held responsible. According to Mahadev Solkar, women in the group started telling the police that "if you are not prepared to release those men, than you should arrest us too, because we are just as innocent as they are." In response, the police told villagers that the men would be produced before the court and whatever the court decided would stand. Nevertheless, the police released Laxman Satley that night.

After Satley was released, the crowd dispersed and returned to the village. The other men spent the night in jail. According to Mahadev Solkar, they were kept in a very dark, small cell and no beds, blankets, or food were provided to them until around 9:00-10:00 the next morning.

On February 19, the men were taken to the judicial magistrate in Chiplun and later released on 1,000 rupees bail each. The Guhagar police told the men that

---

[178] They were charged under Sections 147, 148, 149, 323, 324, 336, 341, and 435 of the Indian Penal Code.

they would have to report to the police station every other day for a month. Police told Solkar that he would be arrested if he did not report to the police station. For the next month, Solkar went to the police station and signed a register as proof of his appearance.

After eight days, the police charged the men with rioting, rioting with a deadly weapon, unlawful assembly, causing hurt, causing hurt with a deadly weapon, reckless endangerment, wrongful restraint, and arson under the Indian Penal Code.[179] They were going to be rearrested, so their lawyer came to the police station and then went to the *tehisildar* (the senior government official at the taluka level) and arranged for the defendants to produce their house ownership papers to the tehisildar, which in effect, made their houses a bail bond.

Solkar told us his opinion of the incident:

> The police arrest people in local communities to harass and demoralize them from agitating against Enron. The police keep tabs on villages and hamlets against the project. Whenever something happens that warrants arrest, these villages are targeted.
>
> Mentally, this whole event has put me completely off balance. It has affected my job, because every time there is a court date, I have to go to Chiplun, which is six hours away and costs 300 to 400 rupees per trip. Earlier the lawyers would take care of it, but now I have to go in person. My finances are affected: I lost work for a month when I had to report to the police station and have lost work for subsequent trips. I am maintaining my innocence, but one never knows. Before this I had never even been to a police station or the courts. Personally, it has cost us 10,000 rupees a person so far, and my monthly salary is only about 3,500 to 4,000 rupees.[180]

The charges filed against the men carry a maximum sentence of up to seven years' imprisonment. The case came up for hearing on January 5, 1998 and was adjourned until March 1998. As of October 1998, the case was still pending.

Dattaram Jangli, who has also been subjected to externment orders for his participation in protests against the Dabhol Power project, and other villagers were

---

[179] They were charged under Sections 147, 148, 149, 323, 324, 336, 341, and 435 of the Indian Penal Code.

[180] Human Rights Watch interview with Mahadev Pandurang Solkar, Bombay, February 6, 1998.

arrested relative to damage to the vehicles of DPC contractors on June 14, 1996, while they attended a village meeting to discuss cleaning a community pond so that it could be used for drinking and other purposes.

While the meeting was going on, Assistant Sub-Inspector P.G. Satoshe arrived, accompanied by seventeen police officers who surrounded the community hall. According to Jangli:

> Satoshe asked people who the village leaders were. He said that senior police officials from Ratnagiri have come to discuss something. When we asked them what this was in regard to, Satoshe said, "You will know when you meet the officials."[181]

Because the police did not specify their reasons for summoning these people, the villagers refused to go meet with them. The police then arrested fifteen villagers and transported them to the Guhagar police station, where their names, addresses, addictions/vices, fingerprints, and any identifiable body marks were recorded.

A few hours later, around 11:00 a.m., the detained villagers were taken to Chiplun and presented to the judicial magistrate, who released them on personal bonds. The cases, however, are pending and villagers are still unclear about the charges leveled against them. Later, they learned that they were charged with vandalizing the vehicle of an Enron contractor. Jangli told us:

> The police are only out to harass us in some way or another, so that we stop our opposition to Enron. But we have lost everything. Everything other than our houses has been taken away. We already face a shortage of fuelwood and green material to fertilize our fields.[182]

Regarding disputes with DPC contractors and police

The biased use of the Indian Penal Code further exacerbates existing tensions between villagers opposed to the Dabhol Power project and those who support it. The tensions, however, began with the types of activities the company engaged in to foster support for the project—such as awarding labor contracts and giving

---

[181] Human Rights Watch interview with Dattaram Jangli, Borbatlewadi village, February 15, 1998.
[182] Ibid.

development funding to individuals to create their own nongovernmental organizations (NGOs).

In the December 11, 1997 issue of the *Far Eastern Economic Review*, an article described Enron's management of local opposition to the project. The article, quoting the chief executive officer of the Enron Power Development Corporation, Rebecca Mark, stated:

> Enron worked to defuse accusations that the company deprived locals of land, and headed off the formation of a powerful lobby against it. It did so in part by involving locals in community activities meant to help people adversely affected by the project, even giving jobs to some. Mark denies the company bought off local people for the sake of peace. "There are always ways to include people, to make them productive when they could be counterproductive. That's not corruption, that's economic interest."[183]

According to the Center for Holistic Studies, this process began in late 1994 when Sanjeev Khandekar, the Dabhol Power Corporation's vice president for community relations, began to offer opponents of the project labor contracts and development funding. A letter to Enron, written by the Center for Holistic Studies, detailed the situation:

> Before the arrival of DPC in the region, there was only one organization engaged in some social work in the area, and that was Shramik Sahayog. It has always been opposed to the project. Others were formed with the efforts of DPC Vice President for Community Relations, Sanjeev Khandekar. According to the villagers, the NGOs are fronts for the Company's handful of supporters in every village.[184]

Sadanand Pawar told Human Rights Watch that from March through May 1997, he was repeatedly offered contracts by Sanjeev Khandekar, individual contractors, and even a local member of the Legislative Assembly (who had a contract of his own with DPC, a clear conflict of interest) as an inducement to stop demonstrating against the project. Pawar said:

---

[183] Shiraz Sidhwa, "Alive and Well: Against the Odds, Enron Makes a Go of It in India," *Far Eastern Economic Review*, December 11, 1997.

[184] Letter from the Center for Holistic Studies to the Enron Corporation in response to Enron's letter to Amnesty International, November 20, 1997.

> [Sanjeev] Khandekar offered us contracts. I would get messages sent through contractors. They repeatedly offered me contracts throughout 1996-1997. They would call me and say, "Take a contract, give work orders, and give up the agitation..." Throughout the agitation, they constantly offered me contracts. One person, Vaishali Patil, was asked by Circle Inspector Desmukh to stop protesting and to take a contract. He [said he] would go with her to Khandekar's and get a contract. This is how people defected... In December 1997, one man, a local Congress MLA [Member of the Legislative Assembly], approached me and said that if I go to Sanjeev Khandekar and take contracts, I will get whatever I want and he will give me contracts. DPC told people that "whoever brings those people in [leaders of the DPC protests] will get contracts."[185]

Pawar also cited Vinay Natu, a BJP MLA as one who took DPC contracts following alleged prompting by the BJP to stop protesting once the project was renegotiated.

According to Pawar and others, the flip-side of contract offers was strong-arm tactics. Pawar told Human Rights Watch:

> When we refused [to accept contracts], the police started their crackdown. Starting in March 1997, whenever there was a police crackdown, four people, including a local MLA would say "Give up the agitation, take a contract, whatever you want we'll give you. If you don't listen, you will face the consequences."

> Any person who honestly opposed the project was destined for jail... They [the police] never harassed contractors, only local workers...Whenever the agitation was in full swing, one leader would defect. For example, Vinay Natu, a BJP MLA, Sushil Velhal, and others would defect and take DPC contracts. Because the BJP controlled them, they could be manipulated. These people were never harassed by the police.[186]

---

[185] Human Rights Watch interview with Sadanand Pawar.
[186] Ibid.

Sushil Velhal, a member of the BJP and a former participant in demonstrations against the project, was one person many individuals cited as an example of the relationship between the company and its contractors. Velhal received contracts as well as development funds from DPC. According to Mangesh Chavan:

> They [DPC] have "fronted" what are local NGOs/contractors who have dubious records as their public examples of community development and working with NGOs... Velhal was boycotted by the local community, he was a known bootlegger and smuggler. Following the Bombay blasts, he was arrested under TADA.[187] He was alleged to have smuggled the RDX [explosives] used in the blasts into the country. All his associates are in jail, and he was heavily surveilled by Customs because of his smuggling activities. In 1995, he started the Guhagar Parishad Vikas Manch, an NGO that he used as a front for his contracting (and possibly illicit activities). Enron associated with him to show they were working with NGOs and had community support; they gave him an ambulance to show they were involved in "community development." Enron gave him other civil contracts as well.[188]

Reputational issues notwithstanding, publications issued by the Dabhol Power Corporation and newspaper reports confirm what many people reported—that Velhal associated with senior officials of the Dabhol Power Corporation and was portrayed as an NGO working with the company. In one case he was photographed with Sanjiv Khandekar, a vice president of DPC, as they inaugurated the Guhagar-Khandwadi bus service.[189] The company also reported that it supported medical check-ups for women on April 27, 1997, which were co-sponsored by the Guhagar Parisar Vikas Manch, Velhal's NGO.[190]

This sort of partnership carries risks, however. On December 9, 1997, Velhal and others stopped Khandekar's car as he was on his way to attend a concert and

---

[187] The Bombay serial bomb blasts took place in 1992 when a series of explosions killed several hundred people. The blasts were attributed to underworld figures in Bombay. TADA was the Terrorist and Disruptive Activities law that imposed draconian anti-terrorism legislation throughout the country.

[188] Human Rights Watch interview with Mangesh Chavan.

[189] *Dabhol Samvad*: *The Monthly Bulletin of the Dabhol Power Company*, Vol. 1, No. 2, March 1997, p. 2.

[190] *Dabhol Samvad...*, Vol. 1, No. 3, April 1997, p. 6.

attacked him. Khandekar told *The Indian Express* that the attack was prompted by his refusal to award a contract to Velhal.[191] In a letter to the Enron Corporation, the Center for Holistic Studies detailed the incident and Velhal's alleged background:

> The DPC Vice-President [Sanjeev Khandekar], his secretary, and the Project Development Officer were badly beaten and their faces blackened by one such "social worker," Sushil Velhal, who heads a DPC-promoted NGO, Guhagar Parisar Vikas Manch... The NGO was formed in late 1994 after Velhal officially announced that he was quitting the anti-Enron agitation and joining hands with DPC. This was after the land acquisition was completed and DPC was desperate to cultivate elements who would support the project in Guhagar taluka, attract people from far away villages to join as laborers and make DPC look more respectable.[192]

Velhal's assault on Khandekar is unique for two reasons: it is the only known case of a contractor attacking a DPC representative and it is the only case in which a contractor has, to our knowledge, been prosecuted for a criminal assault.

Criminal activity, however, was not unique to Velhal. In fact, in a series of incidents going back to 1996, contractors have threatened or assaulted villagers opposed to the project, or damaged their property. The police, in turn, refused to entertain complaints by the victims. Similarly, following disputes between contractors and villagers, police arrested, beat, and detained villagers in retaliation.

For example, on November 22, 1996, police at the Guhagar police station refused to accept the complaint of Sushant Sudhakar Bhatkar. Bhatkar was allegedly assaulted by Sandesh Pundalik Kalgutkar, a local contractor for the Dabhol Power Corporation. According to Bhatkar, on November 22 Kalgutkar left the DPC site, took a sword from his van, and attacked Bhatkar, Sakharam Misal, and Anil Narayan. Bhatkar was injured and, when he lodged a complaint, police told him that the sub-inspector was unavailable to accept the complaint. Thus, they never filed it.[193]

---

[191] "Guhagar Residents Assault Enron Officials," The Indian Express, December 12, 1997.

[192] Letter from the Center for Holistic Studies to the Enron Corporation.

[193] This offence is classified as "voluntary hurt" under Section 324 of the Indian Penal Code and carries a sentence of up to three years' imprisonment. Section 324 of the Indian Penal Code states: "Whoever, except in the case provided for by section 334, voluntarily

On February 27, 1997, police refused to accept the complaint of Adinath Kaljunkar, a participant in protests from the village of Aareygon who had been arrested the previous month under Section 151 of the Code of Criminal Procedure. Kaljunkar telephoned the Guhagar police station on the evening of February 27 and alleged that Deepak Kangutkar, a contractor for DPC, and four other men had threatened to murder him. Kangutkar and the others were DPC contractors and, according to Kaljunkar, believed they would suffer financial losses if the protests continued. The officer refused to send anyone to investigate the complaint. The next morning, February 28, Kaljunkar went to the police station to complain in person. The officer on duty determined that the matter did not warrant further investigation.[194]

Sadanand Pawar received anonymous death threats over the telephone throughout 1997 and early 1998. The caller or callers ordered him to cease his opposition to the Dabhol Power project or face the consequences. Pawar told Human Rights Watch:

> I got threats. Even in December 1997, I got a phone call and an unknown person said "Give up the anti-Enron agitation or you will be killed." This happened around 11:00 p.m. It came from Bombay or outside because the long distance ring is different than the local ring. Before, on three separate occasions, in October [1997], when I was not around, my wife received similar calls.[195]

Pawar told us that he continued to receive anonymous death threats over the phone in the first two months of 1998.[196]

---

causes hurt by means of any instrument for shooting, stabbing, or cutting, or any instrument which, used as a weapon of offence, is likely to cause death, or by means of fire or any means of any explosive substance, or by means of any substance which is deleterious to the human body to inhale, to swallow or to receive into the blood, or by means of any animal, shall be punished with imprisonment of either description for a term which may extend to three years, or with fine, or both."

[194] "In the Service of a Multinational...," pp. 17-18. A death threat is defined as "criminal intimidation" under Section 503 of the Indian Penal Code and is punishable with up to two years' imprisonment.

[195] Human Rights Watch interview with Sadanand Pawar.

[196] An anonymous death threat is considered criminal intimidation under sections 506 and 507 of the Indian Penal Code and is punishable with up to nine years' imprisonment. Section 507 is prosecuted with Section 506 of the Indian Penal Code, which provides up to seven years' imprisonment for committing criminal intimidation. Section 507 of the Indian

Katalwadi Village: April 1997

A particularly serious attack occurred in the village of Katalwadi, where supporters of the company assaulted villagers who were opposed to the project on April 1, 1997. Following the attack, the police arrested and charged the anti-Enron villagers with criminal offenses, including attempted murder, under the Indian Penal Code. The perpetrators of the attack, however, were detained only briefly the following day and were not charged with assault. The details of the case are provided below, as they offer a portrait of tensions at the village level.

The village of Katalwadi is at the forefront of protests against the Dabhol Power project and, according to Anand Arjun Bhuvad, a shop owner and recognized village leader, "Ninety-nine percent of the village is against the project."[197] S.D. Khare, who has been closely involved in the issue and has helped villagers with their legal proceedings due to arrests, told Human Rights Watch, "Kathalwadi has about 225 houses, and only seven houses out of 225 are pro-Enron. Their leader is Mr. Dilip Bane. He is appointed as a labor contractor to Enron."[198] Villagers and other observers told us that the company had "cultivated" these families in order to show that the project had support in surrounding villages.[199]

In response to the activities of Bane and other pro-Enron villagers, and as a sign of community solidarity, the anti-Enron villagers ostracized them by initiating a "social boycott." That is, the pro-Enron villagers were excluded from the major decision-making of the village, prohibited from participating in village-level festivals and ceremonies, and generally excluded from community activities.

The conflict came to a violent climax on April 1, 1997, during the last two days of the Holi festival. The annual festival is celebrated over fifteen to twenty days and, according to village custom, a statue representing the village goddess, Uttararaaj Kaleshwari, is paraded around the village followed by a procession of residents. Devotees lift the goddess and dance with her. In 1997, villagers who

---

Penal Code states: "Whoever commits the offence of criminal intimidation by an anonymous communication, or having taken precaution to conceal the name or abode of the person from whom the threat comes, shall be punished with imprisonment of either description for a term which may extend to two years, in addition to the punishment provided for the offence by Section 506."

[197] Human Rights Watch interview with Anand Arjun Bhuvad, Kathalwadi village, February 15, 1998.
[198] Human Rights Watch interview with S.D. Khare, Guhagar, February 14 1998.
[199] Human Rights Watch interview with Anand Arjun Bhuvad.

were Enron supporters had been banned from participation in the festival as part of the social boycott.

At approximately 6:00 p.m., six of the Enron supporters led by Dilip Bane and his brother Ashok Bane intercepted the procession.[200] They were armed with swords, sharpened hoes (colloquially known as "choppers"), wooden sticks, acid-bulbs, and soda bottles. Acid-bulbs are light bulbs or glass bottles filled with acid which are thrown at people in order to inflict burns and cuts from the broken glass; soda-bottles serve the same function when they are shaken and thrown: the force caused by the carbonated liquid creates an explosion of glass when the bottle strikes an object.

The armed men insisted they be allowed to dance with the deity. Villagers refused because of the social boycott. Ashok Padyal told us:

> They knew fully well that situation was not possible because of the social boycott imposed on them by the entire village because they support Enron. People... said that if they still wanted to participate, they should ask the whole village and let it be a collective decision on whether they could participate.[201]

Following the exchange, the Banes and their associates attacked two of the villagers, Ashok Padyal and his uncle Harishchandra Devale, with their weapons. Padyal told us:

> They knew the village would not allow them to comply, so they started attacking people. When the talking stopped, Ashok, Dilip, and Chandrakant Bane came forward and signaled the others to approach.[202]

The men began by beating Ashok Padyal's uncle, Harishchandra Devale, with bamboo sticks and knocking him to the ground. Then Ashok Bane took a swing

---

[200] According to villagers, the other men with Ashok Bane were, his brother, Dilip Bane, an Enron labor contractor; Chandrakant Bane, a relative of theirs; Ashok Bait; Rajendra Durogoli; Sandeep Bagwe; Dinesh Bait; Hari Kansare, Gorakh Bagawe, and Santosh Bhuvad all came out of Devale's house around the same time. Chandrakant Bane was recognized by DPC as a local Shiv Sena leader and is pictured with Sanjeev Khandekar in the May 1997 issue of *Dabhol Samvad: the Monthly Bulletin of the Dabhol Power Company.*

[201] Human Rights Watch interview with Ashok Padyal, Bombay, February 19, 1998.
[202] Ibid.

at Devale with a sword, missing him. At this point, Ashok Padyal intervened. The missed sword blow at Devale hit Padyal on the neck and elbow. Padyal fell down and was then beaten with bamboo sticks. The assailants went to Devale's house and returned with more acid-bulbs and soda bottles which they threw at villagers in the procession.[203] According to Padyal:

> The distance from where I was beaten to Bane's house is about fifty meters. People started chasing them [the assailants] and then they started throwing soda bottles and acid-bulbs at those in pursuit. The ground is hard, so the impact of soda bottles and acid-bulbs is explosive. This kept people from chasing them. It caused injuries to women, primarily their legs and burned saris. Because they were wearing saris, it was harder for them to avoid the explosions. Lata Pate, Kunda Bane, Rukmini Bagwe, and another woman were injured. I was writhing in pain at the time.[204]

After the attack, as another villager, Anand Arjun Bhuvad, described it:

> The villagers gathered, and the Enron supporters ran into the forest. While they fled, they threw soda-water bottles at people. They also threw acid-bulbs. There were a few injuries for those chasing them. They escaped, though, through the forest to Enron's fuel jetty complex and Konvel.[205]

In anticipation of another attack, some of the residents moved their families into the center of the village. Later, people apprehended another pro-Enron villager, Shankar Bhuvad, an elderly resident whose family was subject to the social boycott. Although his entire family was at home and he did not participate in the attack, villagers yelled and pushed him. Bhuvad told us that he protested to the hostile villagers that the perpetrators knew he would not have approved of the attack, so they had not informed him in advance.[206]

At the same time, twenty to twenty-five villagers gathered to help Ashok Padyal and his uncle. Padyal was taken home, while his uncle was taken to his

---

[203] Ibid.

[204] Ibid.

[205] Human Rights Watch interview with Anand Arjun Bhuvad. Konvel is the village where the fuel complex for the Dabhol Power project is located.

[206] Ibid.

residence—about a five-minute walk away. Between 7:30 and 8:00 p.m. their wounds were treated and dressed, and they were given water and tea at Ramachandra Bhuvad's home. They stayed for ten to fifteen minutes and went home. At Ramachandra Bhuvad's home, senior members of the village discussed how they should respond and decided that they should go to Guhagar government hospital the next morning and tell the police. Padyal told us that, "There was hatred in my mind about those people. I already felt the motive behind the attack was because we are anti-Enron."[207]

The next day, Devale and Padyal, along with Padyal's father, uncle, and cousin, took the 8:00 a.m. bus to Guhagar. The men went to S.D. Khare's house and drafted a complaint between 8:30 and 11:00 a.m., and took it to the hospital. Padyal required stitches on the elbow and a dressing on the neck.

At around 2:00 p.m., police took Ashok Padyal and his father to the station. His uncle and cousin stayed at the hospital because, according to Padyal, "They thought they may be arrested since the police did not like the anti-Enron members of the village."[208]

Meanwhile, in Kathalwadi village, the police came to inquire about the incidents of April 1. But they were not acting on Padyal's complaint. To the contrary, the police came to investigate a complaint filed by the pro-Enron attackers, who claimed that they had been attacked by anti-Enron villagers. Their complaint listed eighteen people who were known as village leaders and participants in the anti-Dabhol Power project protests. When the police came, they called out the names of eighteen men. Four women who had been injured (by the acid-bulbs) the previous day complained to the police about attack and their subsequent injuries. According to one villager:

> [Circle Inspector] Desmukh agreed to take them to the government hospital for an examination. [But] instead of a medical check-up, the women were charged with criminal offences, including attempted murder. They used the incident against Shankar Bhuvad as the reason to charge people with attempted murder. We were taken around noon on April 2 to the Guhagar police station. The four women were put in the lockup as well.[209]

---

[207] Human Rights Watch interview with Ashok Padyal.
[208] Ibid.
[209] Human Rights Watch interview with Anand Arjun Bhuvad.

Once he left the hospital, Padyal went to the Guhagar police station to submit the complaint he had drafted earlier in the day. There he learned that villagers had been arrested and that police were skeptical of his complaint. He told us:

> I gave my written complaint to the police, but the police refused to accept it. Instead, they asked me to narrate the whole incident and how it took place, with every minute detail. After the police took the complaint, I was supposed to sign it. When I read it, I saw that the police had taken a "rough sketch" of the incident and most of the crucial details were missing. There was no mention of the soda bottles and acid- bulbs, no mention of injuries to women, and no mention of swords or other weapons.[210]

Although Padyal was in a great deal of pain because of his injuries, he chose to wait for Circle Inspector Desmukh to amend the complaint.[211] While he waited, police lectured Padyal about the project and their opinion of villagers' opposition, encouraging him to stop protesting. Padyal told us:

> They said, "Why are you opposing the project—it won't be of any benefit to you or any use. It's no use going against the government, they will complete the project by force. You should accept compensation for your land and take whatever benefits the company and government give you. You could get jobs in the project... Just take the jobs."
>
> I asked them how many jobs were there. They said about 200 to 250. I told them that the number of people who will lose land is much more than 200 to 250. I said, "What is the use of all that? If we have land, we can grow crops, graze, implement horticulture. Without land, we can do nothing." They told me, "What's the use? The government will forcibly help Enron complete the project..."
>
> Where was the need of policemen to lecture us about Enron? They must have come to know that the fight in the village was related to Enron. The police were government servants, why did they not lecture the pro-

---

[210] Human Rights Watch interview with Ashok Padyal.
[211] Ibid.

Enron people for attacking us? It is not their job. From what I can tell, there is clear connivance between the police and Enron, and the police are paid to take sides.[212]

Padyal waited until 4:30 p.m. for Desmukh, but he never arrived. Because he was in pain and had missed the bus to his village, Padyal signed the incomplete complaint and managed to obtain a private vehicle to return home.

Twenty villagers who had been attacked were charged with many offences, including rioting, rioting with deadly weapons, unlawful assembly, attempted murder, causing hurt, causing hurt with a deadly weapon or corrosive substance, reckless endangerment, criminal mischief, trespassing, and criminal intimidation.[213] All but two were kept in custody until April 19, and the others were released on April 21. The charges carry very severe penalties: attempted murder, for example, can be punished with life imprisonment. As of October 1998, the cases were still pending.

The Banes and their associates, however, were charged under Section 37 of the Bombay Police Act and released on bail the same day. Following the incident, fifteen to twenty State Reserve Police were stationed in Kathalwadi for a month and remained there until May 1997.

As we have described above, police have assaulted and arbitrarily detained individuals known to oppose the Dabhol Power project. In many cases, these abuses have been directed at groups of demonstrators or, as in the case of Medha Patkar and other NAPM members, have followed from externment orders. But police have also singled out specific individuals for physical reprisal following disputes between anti-Enron villagers and pro-Enron contractors or laborers. Two cases are described below. Following both incidents, the villagers—the victims of the attack—were charged with offences under the Indian Penal Code.

Sanjay Pawar: February 1997

Sanjay Pawar was beaten by State Reserve Police officers following a quarrel with local contractors on February 17, 1997. Subsequently, was arrested on February 28, 1997 and charged with wrongful restraint, assaulting a public servant, and provoking the police officer to "break the peace" because of the incident on February 17.[214] The charges carry a maximum sentence of up to two years'

---

[212] Ibid.

[213] The villagers were charged under sections 147, 148, 149, 307, 323, 324, 336, 337, 427, 452, 504, 506 of the Indian Penal Code.

[214] Pawar was charged under sections 341, 353, and 504 of the Indian Penal Code.

imprisonment. The case had not been resolved as of October 1998. To our knowledge, no police officer has been investigated or charged for assaulting Pawar.

According to Pawar, he participated in the January 30, 1997 protest, and whenever people from the village participated in demonstrations against the project, he would join. Pawar told Human Rights Watch:

> I don't want Enron because of the pollution and the cost escalations of essential commodities, like electricity. There is also the way they take land. Our village could face displacement because of Phase II.[215]

According to Pawar, the incident began over a dispute not overtly linked to opposition against the power project. At approximately 10:00 a.m. on February 17, 1997, while Pawar was working for a road construction firm that is building roads from Guhagar village to the Dabhol Power project site, three or four tankers carrying water, followed by a truck containing officers from the State Reserve Police (SRP), drove past the workers. Pawar flagged down the tankers and asked them to slow down and to leave some water on the road. Since Pawar and others were digging up hard dirt, the water would have softened the ground and made their work easier. The drivers disagreed, told Pawar that he was obstructing them and slowing them down on purpose, and said they could drive as they pleased.

Following that exchange, the SRP officer-in-charge got out of the truck and asked Pawar why he had stopped the tankers. When Pawar explained the situation, the officer started yelling at him, then struck him repeatedly with a lathi. The force of the beating was so severe that the lathi broke over Pawar's head. Pawar told Human Rights Watch:

> I collapsed, and the SRP continued to beat me with their fists and boots. They put me in the SRP van, and the SRP in charge kicked me. About twenty-five to thirty of my coworkers tried to intervene to keep them from putting me in the van, but the police told them to leave or they would deal with them.[216]

The police took Pawar to the infirmary at the DPC project site. His head wound, which required stitches, was treated by the company doctor. Within an

---

[215] Human Rights Watch interview with Sanjay Pawar, Veldur village, February 14, 1998.

[216] Ibid.

hour of the assault, news of Pawar's beating had spread around the community; approximately 200 villagers blocked the road near the project and demanded his release. Concerned about his being on company premises in police hands, villagers wanted him treated at a government hospital and not at the company's infirmary.

When the local police heard about the roadblock, Assistant Sub-Inspector Satoshe and Circle Inspector Desmukh came to the site. The villagers told them what had happened and said that they would not let traffic pass until Pawar was released. A few hours later, around 2:00 p.m., Mangesh Pawar and Sadanand Pawar (no relation) were allowed to take Sanjay Pawar from the site.

Later that afternoon, villagers had a procession, led by former High Court Justice B.G. Kolse-Patil, demanding that police officers leave the Dabhol Power project site and that local businesses cancel their contracts with DPC in protest. The procession ended a few hours later, and villagers dispersed.

On the morning of February 28, Mangesh Pawar and Sadanand Pawar were served with prohibitory orders and arrested and Sanjay Pawar was arrested for assaulting an SRP officer.[217] Sanjay Pawar told Human Rights Watch:

> I was on leave from February 17 to 20 because of my injuries. On the 28th, I was back at work when Circle Inspector Desmukh arrested me around 8:30. He didn't tell me anything, just took me to the lockup at Guhagar. I had no idea why I was grabbed. I was in the lockup for over an hour; Judge Kolse-Patil was there as well. We were taken to [the court at] Chiplun. Kolse-Patil was charged for violating prohibitory orders and causing obstruction.[218]

Commenting on his experience, Pawar said, "Security is given only to the company—never to the people."[219]

In the meantime, a broader crackdown was occurring. Later on February 28, while protesting police excesses, several hundred protesters from surrounding villages participated in a hunger strike at the Guhagar police station. They were arrested for violating Section 37 of the Bombay Police Act, and some of the participants were beaten by police. One protester, Surendra Thatte, told Human Rights Watch:

---

[217] Police viewed Sadanand Pawar and Mangesh Pawar as leaders of demonstrations against the Dabhol Power project. See above.
[218] Human Rights Watch interview with Sanjay Pawar.
[219] Ibid.

I was arrested on February 28, 1997. This was during a fast with Medha Patkar to protest at the police station with about 500 other people. Around 11:30 a.m., the police arrested about 225 people. We were shouting slogans, singing songs, and giving speeches when they arrested us. We were going to leave around 4:00 p.m., but they arrested us instead. They beat people with lathis and threw people in police vans, very brutal. Then they took them to Chiplun and presented them before the magistrate. In protest, people refused to post a personal bond and were jailed.[220]

The cases against protesters were still pending as of October 1998.

Veldur raid: June 1997

A further incident, prompted by a heated argument and unarmed scuffle between DPC laborers, villagers opposed to the project, and the police occurred on June 2 and 3, 1997, less than a week after Medha Patkar and other activists were arrested, beaten, and detained by police. Following the incident on June 2, the police launched a raid on the village of Veldur. The police beat villagers, then arrested twenty-six women and thirteen men.

On June 2, 1997, as DPC laborers went through Veldur village on their way to the Enron site, they confronted villagers who were opposed to the project. Local residents did not want them to pass through the village because they worked for DPC. A shouting match and some minor scuffles ensued between the two parties. Villagers reported that the workers were verbally abusive and threatening them.[221]

Although the villagers were unarmed, the laborers left and returned with a police escort, comprising eleven male and two female officers. More arguments and scuffles took place. During the argument, one of the female police officers, R.P. Nachankar, slapped sixteen-year-old Sugandha Vasudev Bhalekar, which caused an altercation between some of the villagers and the police women.[222] Officer Nachankar's sari was partially stripped. Then, Police Sub-Inspector Waman Janu ordered the police to fire one round in the air, after which the crowd dispersed.[223] The laborers passed through the village and went to the site of the project.

---

[220] Human Rights Watch interview with Surendra Thatte.
[221] Committee for Peoples' Democratic Rights, "Say Yes to Enron: Police Coercion and Popular Resistance," July 1997, Bombay, p. 2.
[222] Ibid., p. 3.
[223] Ibid., pp. 3-4.

Early in the morning on June 3, the Maharashtra Police and the Special Reserve Police Force launched a raid on the village of Veldur. At approximately 6:00 a.m., eight vans of the State Reserve Police Force and three jeeps of Guhagar police entered Veldur village, carrying approximately 135 police officers.[224] According to the Committee for Peoples' Democratic Rights (CPDR), a respected Indian human rights organization, the police divided into groups of ten and began to raid households in the village while arbitrarily beating and arresting villagers. Because of the early hour, most of the adult men had left to go fishing, so the majority of people in the village were women, children, and the elderly. Gangaji Jambhalkar, an elderly fisherman in Veldur who was standing in a small community center adjacent to the jetty on the morning of June 3, told Human Rights Watch:

> On June 2, there was a skirmish over the Enron issue. The next day, I was standing near a shop. The sudden action police took against us was surprising. I was beaten by a lathi on my wrist and fell to the ground. They came down and just started beating people. I have a small two-cylinder boat and use it as a fisherman. I am sixty-five years old and watched them beat people.[225]

One villager, Vithal Padyal, watched the police enter his home, beat his family, and arrest two of his children. Ironically, the young people who were arrested worked for DPC. His account underscores the arbitrariness and brutality of the police. He told Human Rights Watch:

> On the other side of the village, there was a skirmish [on June 2]. The next day, at six in the morning, the police came in vans. They started going around to houses. They came in and first hit my daughter, Madhuri Madhukar Batokar, who was nine months pregnant at the time. She was hit on the back with a lathi. The police tried to hit me, but I said, "Look at my hair" because it is gray and I am old, and they didn't hit me. Then they caught hold of my son Laloo and his brother Ankhosh. They are twenty-one and twins. Both of them worked at the

---

[224] Ibid., p. 4.
[225] Human Rights Watch interview with Gangaji Jambhalkar, Veldur village, February 14, 1998.

DPC site, so they showed the police their ID cards. In spite of showing them the ID cards, the police beat them with lathis.[226]

The twins were taken into custody by the State Reserve Police. According to their father, Circle Inspector Desmukh kept them in custody for six days without producing them for the court. Desmukh asked the young men to give the names of people involved in the skirmish and protests. They were unable to provide this information to police, since they had not been involved in the protests. After six days, they were transferred to the jail at Chiplun and then transferred again to Yerewada jail, where they were imprisoned for another six days.[227]

The police also arrested and detained juveniles during the raid in violation of India's Juvenile Justice Act, which prohibits the detention of males under the age of sixteen and females under the age of eighteen.[228] Ranjana Padyal, a resident of Veldur, described how the police entered her home and began beating her family members and arrested her fourteen-year-old son, Balakrishna Ramesh Padyal:

> They just entered my house, hit my husband with lathis. He works in Bombay and had come home to attend a marriage. They woke up my fourteen-year-old son and told him that he had to come with them... They kept him in custody for thirteen days. They never said what law they had arrested him under, and he was never associated in the protests against the project.[229]

The Peoples' Union for Civil Liberties (PUCL), a respected Indian human rights organization, investigated the incidents at Veldur and reported that several other juveniles had been arrested and detained: among them, sixteen-year-old Sugandha Vasudev Balekar (who had been assaulted by a female police officer the previous day), two sisters, fourteen-year-old Vanita and fifteen-year-old Sanita Patekar, and fifteen-year-old Rakha Kishore Padyal. Police falsely recorded the ages of these minors so that they would be considered adults, and neither the court nor the police attempted to verify their status as juveniles.[230]

---

[226] Human Rights Watch interview with Vithal Padyal.

[227] Ibid.

[228] For a detailed discussion of the Juvenile Justice Act, 1986, see: *Police Abuse and Killings of Street Children in India*, (New York: Human Rights Watch, 1996).

[229] Human Rights Watch interview with Ranjana Padyal, Veldur village, February 14, 1998.

[230] "Report of the Incidents ...," pp. 5-6.

Both the PUCL and the CPDR determined that several women of the village were subjected to exceptionally brutal treatment, in part because their male relatives were recognized leaders of the anti-Enron protests. For example, twenty-four-year-old Sadhana Bhalekar is the wife of Vithal "Baba" Bhalekar, a local fisherman and a recognized protest leader who had been arrested as early as 1994 for demonstrating against the project. On June 3, police armed with batons broke into her home, beat sleeping members of her family, then smashed the window and door of her bathroom while she was taking a bath. Bhalekar, who was three months pregnant at the time, was dragged out of the bathroom, naked, and beaten with batons in her house and on the street. Bhalekar told the CPDR fact-finding team that Assistant Sub-Inspector P.G. Satoshe was present and told police, "This is Baba Bhalekar's wife, bang her head on the road."[231] Bhalekar provided the details of the incident in an affidavit filed with the Chiplun judicial magistrate on June 9, 1997.[232]

Police also beat her polio-stricken and mentally retarded brother-in-law Pradeep Dattatreya Bhalekar and her nephew Anil. In addition, two of her sisters-in-law, Indira Pandurang Madekar and Supriya Chandrakant Padyal, who were staying at the house for a vacation, were dragged outside and beaten.[233] Bhalekar's affidavit to a judicial magistrate states:

> While I was being taken forcibly out of the house to the police van, my one and a half year old daughter held on to me but the police kicked her away. My sisters-in-law, Mrs. Indira Pandurang Medhekar and Mrs. Supriya Chandrakant Padyal had come to their maternal home. Of these, Supriya Chandrakant Padyal was thrown off the loft on to the ground and was beaten with batons and forced into the van. Indira Pandurang Medhekar too was beaten and forced into the van.[234]

Other villagers were similarly beaten. Ambaji Dabholkar told the CPDR fact-finding team that two daughters of Viju Bhalokar were beaten so severely that they began to urinate.[235]

Eight of the villagers formally complained of ill-treatment by police, including Anil Medekar, Supriya Padyal, Sugandha Bhalekar, Anita Beradkar,

---

[231] "Say Yes to Enron...," p. 4.
[232] Affidavit of Sadhana Vithal Bhalekar, June 9, 1997.
[233] "Say Yes to Enron...," pp. 4-5.
[234] Affidavit of Sadhana Vithal Bhalekar.
[235] "Say Yes to Enron...," pp. 4-5.

Sunanda Bhalekar, Sahdana Bhalekar, Sangeeta Bhalekar, and Indira Madekar. The PUCL determined that they had injuries consistent with beating by police batons.[236]

Thirty-nine people—twenty-six of them women—were arrested in the Veldur raid. They were charged under the Indian Penal Code for rioting, rioting with deadly weapons, causing hurt to deter a public servant from his duty, endangering human life, and attempted murder. These charges carry a maximum sentence of life imprisonment.[237] As of October 1998, the charges were pending.

---

[236] "Incidents Occurring from June 2, 1997...," pp. 3-4.
[237] Ibid. Specifically, the police charged villagers under sections 147, 148, 149, 307, 332, 336, 337, 341, 353, and 427 of the Indian Penal Code and Section 135 of the Bombay Police Act.

VI. The Applicable Laws

Leading activists and members of organizations representing villagers opposed to the project have been subjected to repeated short-term detention and abuse in custody by police. Most frequently those detained have been held under laws which provide for preventive detention. In many cases, they have been detained for periods ranging from several days or longer without being produced before a magistrate within twenty-four hours, as required under Indian law. During mass arrests at demonstrations in villages surrounding the project site, protesters have been beaten with canes (*lathis*), or otherwise assaulted by the police, in some cases sustaining severe injuries. Police have also tear-gassed peaceful demonstrations.

Governments have the right to counter any threat to public order. Human Rights Watch is also aware that some of the charges brought against activists associated with opposition to the Dabhol Power Corporation include acts of violence such as stone-throwing or breaching police barricades. However, examining the state's response to opposition to the Dabhol Power Corporation, Human Rights Watch believes that the state government of Maharashtra has engaged in a systematic pattern of suppression of the rights of freedom of expression and peaceful demonstration coupled with arbitrary detentions, and beatings. In addition, police have consistently failed to investigate or prosecute reports of threats against opponents of the Dabhol Power project and have failed to prosecute the perpetrators of attacks on opponents of the Dabhol Power Project. These actions are clearly violations of international human rights law. The police have also misused preventative detention laws to detain people for the peaceful expression of their views. These arrests violate the internationally recognized rights of freedom of expression, peaceful assembly, protection against unjust arrest and detention, and police mistreatment.

International Law

Freedom of expression is protected under Article 19 of the International Covenant on Civil and Political Rights (ICCPR), to which India is a party.[238] In

---

[238] ICCPR, Article 19 states: 1. Everyone shall have the right to hold opinions without interference. 2. Everyone shall have the right to freedom of expression; this right shall include freedom to seek, receive and impart information and ideas of all kinds, regardless of frontiers, either orally, in writing or in print, in the form of art, or through any other media of his choice. 3. The exercise of the rights provided for in paragraph 2 of this article carries with it special duties and responsibilities. It may therefore be subject to certain

particular, the right to receive and impart information has been suppressed under the guise of protecting public order.

Similarly, by invoking sections of the Bombay Police Act, Human Rights Watch believes that the Maharashtra government has engaged in a systematic attempt to suppress the right of peaceful assembly when the reason for assembly is opposition to the Dabhol Power Project. Freedom of assembly is protected under Article 21 of the ICCPR.[239]

Arbitrary and illegal arrests and detention are forbidden by the ICCPR.[240] Illegal arrests and detentions are by definition "arbitrary"; such acts can also be arbitrary if they blatantly contravene international standards of human rights and procedural fairness, regardless of specific provisions of domestic law. Basic procedural rights of persons who are arrested include the right to know the reasons for arrest, the right to be brought promptly before a judge or other judicial officer following arrest, and the right to receive a trial in a reasonable time or release.[241] Victims of unlawful arrest also have an enforceable right to compensation.[242]

Police beatings of protesters and villagers demonstrating against the Dabhol Power project blatantly contravene the United Nations Code of Conduct for Law Enforcement Officials and the United Nations Basic Principles on the Use of Force and Firearms by Law Enforcement Officials. The U.N. Code of Conduct for Law Enforcement Officials outlines strict guidelines defining when the use of force is acceptable conduct. Article 3 of the code states that "Law enforcement officials may use force only when strictly necessary and to the extent required for the performance of their duty." Under the code, use of force must be determined by the "principle of proportionality," and in no case should force be used which is disproportionate to the final objective of law enforcement officials.[243] Similarly,

---

restrictions, but these shall only be such as are provided by law and are necessary: (a) For respect of the rights or reputations of others; (b) For the protection of national security or of public order (ordre public), or of public health or morals.

[239] ICCPR, Article 21 states: The right of peaceful assembly shall be recognized. No restrictions may be placed on the exercise of this right other than those imposed in conformity with the law and which are necessary in a democratic society in the interests of national security or public safety, public order (ordre public), the protection of public health or morals or the protection of the rights and freedoms of others.

[240] ICCPR, Article 9 prohibits arbitrary arrest or detention, and Article 9(5) mandates that "Anyone who has been the victim of unlawful arrest or detention shall have an enforceable right to compensation;

[241] ICCPR, Article 9(2), 9(3), and 9(4).

[242] ICCPR, Article 9(5).

[243] United Nations Code of Conduct for Law Enforcement Officials, Article 3.

the United Nations Basic Principles on the Use of Force and Firearms by Law Enforcement Officials states that the use of force should be proportional to the "seriousness of the offence and the legitimate objective to be achieved" and requires law enforcement officials to "minimize damage and injury."[244] Moreover, Section 13 of the principles states that use of force is only acceptable when policing unlawful assemblies, and in such cases stringent guidelines apply. Section 13 of the principles states that during unlawful, but nonviolent assemblies police "shall avoid the use of force or, where that is not practicable, shall restrict such force to the minimum extent necessary."[245]

The Laws of India

Article 19 of the Constitution of the Republic of India protects freedom of speech, expression, peaceful assembly, association, and movement. It permits restriction of these rights in order to maintain the public order, provided that the restrictions are "reasonable."

In the case of imposition of Section 37 of the Bombay Police Act in order to restrict freedom of expression and peaceful assembly, the Supreme Court of India has outlined four rules to determine whether the imposition of the law is a violation of Article 19 of the constitution. The criteria are cumulative and concurrent so that all conditions must be satisfied in order to justify a legal prohibition on freedom of expression and peaceful assembly.[246] The most important aspect of the test is determining whether the legal restriction of rights enshrined in Article 19 is reasonable. The court devised a "the test of reasonableness" which stipulates that the court must determine "whether the law strikes a proper balance between social control on the one hand and the rights of the individual on the other hand."[247]

---

[244] United Nations Basic Principles on the Use of Force and Firearms by Law Enforcement Officials, Section 5(a) and 5(b).

[245] United Nations Basic Principles on the Use of Force and Firearms by Law Enforcement Officials, Section 13.

[246] The specified rules are: (a) Whether the law imposes a restriction on the freedom in question; (b) Whether the restrictions have been imposed by law; (c) Whether the restrictions are reasonable; and (d) Whether the restriction, besides being, reasonable, is imposed for one of the specified clauses (2) to (6) of the article. Clauses (2) to (6) of Article 19 define the conditions under which laws can be imposed to restrict freedom of expression and peaceful assembly and include restrictions to protect public order or public morality, to protect the Scheduled Tribes, or to ensure operation of State-owned enterprises.

[247] In order to determine the reasonableness of the law, the Supreme Court devised test criteria. The test criteria are: (a) the nature of the right infringed; (b) underlying purpose of the restriction imposed; (c) evil sought to be remedied by the law, its extent and urgency;

Article 19 has also been interpreted by the Supreme Court as a protection against prohibitory or externment orders issued under sections 144 and 151 of the Code of Criminal Procedure when they are issued in order to curtail freedom of movement. The court has ruled that an individual must be allowed a hearing before such an order is issued. In order to adhere to Article 19, the police must allow a hearing on the order, before the order is issued.

Article 21 of the Indian constitution provide safeguards against arbitrary arrest or detention. The Supreme Court has ruled that raids similar to the police raid in Veldur on June 3, 1997, are unconstitutional because they violate Article 21. In addition, the Supreme Court has ruled in five decisions that Article 21 of the Indian constitution forbids torture, although the constitutional prohibition is not explicit.[248]

Article 22 of the Indian Constitution and sections 50, 56, 57, and 70 of the Code of Criminal Procedure specify that an arrested person must be told the reason for his or her arrest, and must be presented before a magistrate within twenty-four hours; otherwise the detention is illegal. To detain a person for a period longer than twenty-four hours, the police must obtain permission from a magistrate.

(d) how far the restriction is or is not proportionate to the evil; and (e) prevailing conditions at the time.

[248] *Sunil Batra v. Delhi Administration*, A.I.R., 1978 S.C. 1675; *Sunil Batra v. Delhi Administration II*, A.I.R. 1980 S.C. 1579, paragraphs 31 and 42; *Sher Singh v. State of Punjab*, A.I.R. 1983 S.C. 465, paragraph 11; *Javed v. State of Maharashtra*, A.I.R. 1985 S.C. 231, paragraph 4. In *Sita Ram v. State of U.P.*, A.I.R. 1979 S.C. 745, the Supreme Court ruled that: An undertrial or convicted prisoner cannot be subjected to a physical or mental restraint (a) which is not warranted by the punishment awarded by the court, or (b) which is in excess of the requirements of prisoners discipline, or (c) which constitutes human degradation.

VII. Complicity: The Dabhol Power Corporation

There are no international regulations on transnational corporations (TNCs) that oblige them to respect human rights. There have been, however, several attempts by U.N. agencies to develop codes of conduct to ensure that the activities of TNCs do not contribute to human rights violations.

The first international attempt to regulate corporations was the International Labour Organisation's (ILO) adoption of its Tripartite Declaration of Principles for Multinationals and Social Policy in 1977. The principles detailed the responsibilities of TNCs to operate in a manner consistent with international human rights and labor rights laws. Later, in 1986, the United Nations Committee on Transnational Corporations developed its own code of conduct for TNCs. Like the ILO's declaration of principles, the U.N. code of conduct stated that TNCs had a responsibility to respect human rights.

These initiatives, more than a decade old, have been largely ignored. In 1995, however, the recognition that TNCs had a responsibility to respect human rights resurfaced. Unlike the intergovernmental initiatives of the past, this movement was largely driven by nongovernmental organizations (NGOs) based on the perception that governments were unwilling or uninterested in ensuring that corporations were not complicit in human rights violations. While NGO efforts have many disparate foci of attention and are not based on unified doctrine or a guiding document, there are several principles relating to human rights, environmental protection, and equitable economic development that characterize these efforts overall. In the absence of a concerted intergovernmental initiative on this issue, NGOs' research, documentation, and perspectives have set the tone of this international debate.

In May 1998, acceptable corporate conduct was quantified in a survey of NGOs conducted by the University of Notre Dame (Indiana) and Price Waterhouse. The findings were presented to the World Economic Forum in Davos, Switzerland. The survey detailed clear standards for acceptable corporate behavior on issues such as transparency, accountability, working conditions and environmental responsibility. Specifically, more than 90 percent of NGOs surveyed reported that transnational corporations must be responsible for: ensuring proper working conditions, including nondiscrimination; respect for freedom of association and collective bargaining; prohibitions on forced and child labor; complying with national laws; and avoiding illegal or illicit activities such as corruption. Moreover, NGOs stated that the best method to ensure compliance was through independent monitoring of corporate operations and credible reporting by companies to the public.²⁴⁹

NGO investigations and campaigns have had some impact. Two of Enron's competitors in the oil and gas industry, Royal Dutch/Shell and British Petroleum, responded to pressure and criticism of their operations in Nigeria and Colombia, respectively, by acknowledging that human rights should be an integral part of company operations and by formulating human rights policies. Intergovernmental organizations are reexamining the effect of TNCs' activities on human rights, as well. For example, on August 12, 1998, the United Nations Subcommission on the Prevention of Discrimination and Protection of Minorities passed a resolution to set up a committee to study the impact of TNCs on human rights.²⁵⁰

Human Rights Watch believes that corporations have an clear responsibility to avoid complicity in human rights violations. Complicity occurs in several cases. First, when corporations benefit from the failure of government to enforce human rights standards. Second, when corporations are involved in systematic violations of rights and the state, aware of such violations, fails to meet its obligations under international human rights law; this constitutes human rights abuse by state omission and corporate commission. Third, when a corporation facilitates or participates in government human rights violations. Facilitation includes the company's provision of material or financial support for state security forces which then commit human rights violations that benefit the company. In the case of the Dabhol Power project, DPC has facilitated human rights abuses by the state, has benefited from them, and has also benefited from a failure of the government to enforce human rights standards.

As a result of our research, Human Rights Watch believes that the Dabhol Power Corporation—and its parent companies Enron, General Electric, and Bechtel—are complicit in human rights violations by the Maharashtra state government. Human Rights Watch does not take a position on the persistent and pervasive allegations of corruption that surround Enron's establishment in Maharashtra and its way of doing business there. But, as described above, Enron's local entity, the Dabhol Power Corporation, benefited directly from an official policy of suppressing dissent through misuse of the law, harassment of anti-Enron

---

²⁴⁹ Georges Enderle and Glen Peters, *A Strange Affair: the Emerging Relationship Between NGOs and Transnational Companies*, (New York: Price Waterhouse and the University of Notre Dame, 1998), pp. iii-iv.
²⁵⁰ United Nations Subcommission on the Prevention of Discrimination and Protection of Minorities, Resolution E/CN.4/Sub.2/1998/L.3, August 12, 1998.

protest leaders and prominent environmental activists, and police practices ranging from arbitrary to brutal.

As we detail below, DPC's involvement in suppressing dissent was at times more direct, and there can be little question that the company and the police have operated in tandem against the protesters. The Dabhol Power Corporation pays the state forces that committed human rights violations; it provided other material support to these forces; and it failed to act on credible allegations that its own contractors were engaged in criminal activity that rose to the level of human rights violations due to the failure of the state to investigate the crimes.

As early as 1994, the company invoked Section 47 of the Bombay Police Act and entered into a financial arrangement with the state government of Maharashtra for the services of the State Reserve Police officers. DPC disputes that it employs the police, stating:

> [T]he Dabhol Power Company does not employ, second or subcontract police officers at the site. By law, we are required to offset the cost of police officers placed near our site if police officials deem it necessary to preserve law and order when protests occur. We have no authority over their actions.[251]

However, the law itself indicates that the relationship is one in which the company employs the police, although the chain of command remains under state control.

Section 47 of the Bombay Police Act states:

> Employment of additional police on application of a person—(1) The Commissioner or Superintendent may, *on the application of any person*, depute any additional number of Police to keep the peace, to preserve order or to enforce any of the provisions of this or any other Act in respect of any particular class or classes of offences or to perform any other Police duties at any place in the area under his charge. (2) Such additional police shall be employed *at the cost of the person making the application*, but shall be subject to the orders of the Police authorities and shall be employed for such period as the appointing authority thinks fit. (3) If the person upon whose application such additional Police are employed, shall, at any time make a written requisition to the appointing

---

[251] Letter from the Dabhol Power Corporation to Amnesty International, November 17, 1997.

authority to which the application of the employment of additional Police was made, for the withdrawal of the said Police, he shall be relieved from the cost thereof at the expiration of such period not exceeding one month from the date of delivery of such requisition as the State Government or the appointing authority, as the case may be, shall determine. [Emphasis added]

From 1994 to the present, between ten and 300 Maharashtra Police and State Reserve Police Force officers, at any given time, have been stationed at the Dabhol Power Corporation site. The cost is 125 rupees a day per officer stationed at the site. The details of the arrangement were explained to Human Rights Watch by the officer who commands these personnel, Police Sub-Inspector P.G. Satoshe:

> Payment of the officers by the company is based on fixed rates set by the government for every person there. I calculate the number of officers there and according to the rates, submit a report to the superintendent of police [SP] in Ratnagiri. The SP submits the report to the company who pays the government according to the rates. In the last year, there are between ten and one hundred officers stationed at the site, depending on the law and order situation. I do not handle any money. The company pays directly to the government. The police have been there since 1994, when the project started.[252]

These forces committed human rights violations in at least thirty demonstrations in 1997 that Human Rights Watch directly investigated; and they were the personnel stationed at the site when police beat protesters at the company gates on three occasions. Moreover, the State Reserve Police Force, whose only function is to provide security for company property and personnel, have committed abuses outside the scope of demonstrations—against Sanjay Pawar and during the Veldur raid on June 3. The role of these officers was detailed by Sub-Inspector Satoshe:

> There is a combination of Maharashtra Police [MP] and Special Reserve Police [SRP] at the site. Not within the site, but next to it, in their own compound. The SRP are only around to deal with law and order problems, nothing else... These were due to the anti-Enron agitations...

---

[252] Human Rights Watch interview with Sub-Inspector P.G. Satoshe.

The MP deal with crime and other things. The SRP and MP are under my command.[253]

The DPC/police relationship also extends beyond security payments. Several eyewitnesses told Human Rights Watch that a helicopter that was reportedly contracted to the company was used to allow police officers and other state officials to monitor protesters during the January 30, 1997 demonstration. S.D. Khare, who witnessed the demonstrations on January 30, told us:

> Behind the scenes, Enron has done everything to destroy the movement. For example, during the protests of January 30th, a Gulf Air helicopter was permanently used to survey the protesters with the District Collector T. Chandrashekar and the police inside. If someone were interested, they should check the flight manifestos.[254]

Other eyewitnesses have similar recollections of the helicopter during protests. Mangesh Chavan, told us that, "Enron's helicopter was used in 1996-1997 to transport sub-inspectors and to watch local activists. It was used on January 30 and May 20 to survey the area [where protests were occurring] to see if people were approaching the site."[255] Medha Patkar noted that on January 30, "I saw the helicopter with the deputy superintendent of police in it. It was circling overhead. The collector, T. Chandrashekar, was in the helicopter as well. When I was arrested on the scooter, the helicopter was overhead."[256]

The company could not have been ignorant of the human rights abuses committed by police whom it paid; frequently those abuses sparked further protest, company representatives were in contact with government officials, several cases received press attention, there were legal proceedings, and the company had information sources among its contractors in the villages. For example, following the demonstrations in early February 1997 where hundreds of people were arrested, the *Times of India* reported on the morning of February 28 that the government was "certain to come down heavily on the anti-Enron agitation..." because a water pipeline had been damaged a few days earlier. According to the newspaper, officials from the Dabhol Power Corporation had held "an emergency meeting" with representatives of the state government to discuss the protests and the

---

[253] Ibid.
[254] Human Rights Watch interview with S.D. Khare.
[255] Human Rights Watch interview with Mangesh Chavan.
[256] Human Rights Watch interview with Medha Patkar.

government had "reportedly assured the officials that firm measures would be taken against agitators...."[257]

Moreover, DPC and press reports quoting company officials indicate the company was aware of the demonstrations and commented on the protests. But the company did not publicly take a stand for more humane policing on its behalf. Indeed, it blamed anti-Enron villagers for the polarization that took place and viewed their tactics of dissent as illegal. For example, the company published a detailed commentary on the violent protest of January 30, in which isolated incidents of stone-throwing and minor skirmishes took place between protesters and police. *Dabhol Samvad: The Monthly Bulletin of the Dabhol Power Corporation* noted, of that protest:

> [O]ver the past two-and-a-half years we have always been prepared to hold a dialogue with anyone who approaches us in keeping with the democratic tradition. However, this can hardly be said of the groups opposing us. Could it be that they lack our faith in law and democracy? The intimidatory tactics that the opposition is resorting to are not means that can be justified in a society that follows the rule of law.[258]

The company was aware that villagers were arrested for demonstrating against the project. In the May 1997 issue of *Dabhol Samvad*, the company cited the village of Peve as a beneficiary of the company's water programs and noted:

> Two months ago [March 1997], the entire village had participated in the anti-Enron agitation. Some of the women from the village were even arrested by police.[259]

Vrinda Walavalkar, a spokesperson for DPC, following demonstrations against the diversion of villagers' water supply to the company in which hundreds of people were arrested for violating Section 37 of the Bombay Police Act, restated the company's position that demonstrations against the project amounted to criminal activity when she told the *Times of India* that the company had "only

---

[257] Suhas Phadke, "Government May Crackdown on Anti-Enron Agitators," *Times of India*, February 28, 1997.
[258] *Dabhol Samvad...*, Vol. 1, No. 2, p. 1.
[259] *Dabhol Samvad...*, Vol. 1, No. 4, p. 3.

enough water for drinking and cooking purposes... " and that "It is hard to proceed with our schedules if such unlawful methods are used against us."[260]

Commenting on demonstrations that took place in May 1997, the vice-president of the Dabhol Power Corporation told *The Times of India* that the agitators did not know why they were protesting and the company saw this as an issue between the government and the protesters.[261]

Most important, perhaps, is the statement made by the Dabhol Power Corporation to Amnesty International (AI) on November 17, 1997. AI had raised concerns based on the reports of local human rights organizations about abuses committed by police in conjunction with the protest demonstrations against the project. The DPC's letter detailed the company's position on human rights and illustrates its belief that human rights are not the company's problem: "If you have concerns about police actions, we suggest that you take it up with the police or government body that is responsible for their operations."[262]

Finally, the conduct of DPC contractors links the company to a pattern of state tolerance of criminal violence that operated to the DPC's benefit. This report and other reports by Indian human rights organizations contain details of two attacks by contractors on villagers opposed to DPC; one death threat by a contractor and several offers of contracts to a local leader to stop protesting. In response to these allegations, the company wrote:

> We found no evidence of wrongdoing by our employees or contractors...
>
> Dabhol Power Company would not tolerate any human rights abuses by its employees and sub-contractors. They work only within the boundaries and would not have interaction while on-duty with individuals outside the perimeter of the DPC site.[263]

This argument is disingenuous. There is substantial anecdotal evidence that the DPC awarded some contracts on the basis of the recipients' disavowing prior opposition to the project and that such contracts were offered outside the project

---

[260] "Villagers Cut Water Supply to Enron Site," *Times of India*, February 16, 1997.

[261] K.M. Sandeep, "Villagers Extend Lukewarm Support to Anti-Enron Stir," *Times of India*, May 19, 1997.

[262] Letter from the Dabhol Power Corporation to Amnesty International, November 17, 1997.

[263] Ibid.

site. In this respect at least, DPC authorized contractors to act as its agents in the battle of wills surrounding the project. While Human Rights Watch does not have evidence that the company approved of any specific criminal activity by its contractors, the fact that the company sweepingly denied all wrongdoing by its contractors is a shirking of responsibility for actions that directly bear on the company's relations with villages surrounding the site.

VIII. Responsibility: Financing Institutions and the Government of the United States

Human Rights Watch believes that the financiers of Phase I, and the U.S. government agencies involved in lobbying for the project, share responsibility for the human rights violations described above. The U.S. government bears special responsibility because of its forceful, aggressive lobbying on behalf of the three U.S.-based companies developing the project; and because it extended hundreds of millions of dollars in public funds for the project while it was seemingly indifferent to the human rights policies that govern these transactions.

Human Rights Watch also believes that the institutions which agreed to finance Phase II need to implement adequate safeguards to ensure respect for human rights in order to avoid responsibility for human rights violations. In particular, these institutions should demonstrate their clear commitment to respect human rights by addressing the legal prohibitions on freedom of expression and peaceful assembly which are still in force; the fact that many of the cases against activists are still pending; and the fact that the company receiving funding (DPC) has made no attempt to correct its practices and ensure respect for human rights, but rather continues to benefit from the abuses.

In previous reports, Human Rights Watch has called for governmental and private financial institutions to condition financing for projects on measurable compliance with human rights. For example, in 1992, in a report on the Narmada Dam in India, Human Rights Watch called on donor governments "to urge the World Bank to include specific human rights protections in any decision to continue funding" of the project, and "If human rights violations continue, the World Bank should suspend further disbursements of funds for the project."[264] In a 1995 report on the Three Gorges Dam in China, Human Rights Watch recommended that governmental and private institutions should "insist on human rights impact assessment studies before providing any financing, goods or services" and "insist on firm and verifiable guarantees...that human rights will be respected before committing themselves to the project."[265]

In the case of the Dabhol Power project, because of the complexities and numerous actors involved in financing, Human Rights Watch investigated the role

---

[264] "Before the Deluge: Human Rights Abuses at India's Narmada Dam," *A Human Rights Watch Short Report*, Vol. 4, Issue 15, June 17, 1992, p. 3.

[265] "The Three Gorges Dam in China: Forced Resettlement, Suppression of Dissent and Labor Rights Concerns," *A Human Rights Watch Short Report*, Vol. 7, No. 2, February 1995, p. 5.

In the case of the Dabhol Power project, because of the complexities and numerous actors involved in financing, Human Rights Watch investigated the role of financial institutions for Phase I of the project to determine whether any safeguards existed to monitor or condemn human rights violations. We also examined the actors responsible for financing Phase II.

Phase I Financing

When financing for Phase I of the project was planned, the involvement of multilateral development banks, primarily the World Bank, was considered crucial to the project's success. The World Bank, however, refused to fund the project. The World Bank's analysis was telling and reinforces later criticism by protesters that the price of power generated by the project is too high. Specifically, the World Bank did not oppose the privatization of the Indian power sector or the participation of multinationals in power generation, but its experts felt that this particular project was not viable. A letter from Heinz Vergin, the country director for India, to Montek Singh Ahluwalia, the secretary of the Department of Economic Affairs for the Indian Ministry of Finance, states:

> Our analysis based on the parameters provided to us indicates that the LNG [liquefied natural gas]-based project as presently formulated is not economically viable, and thus could not be financed by the Bank. We have reached this conclusion on the following two grounds:
>
> (a) the proposed 2,015 MW project is too large for base load operation in the Maharashtra State Electricity Board (MSEB) system. Project design is inflexible and would result in uneconomic plant dispatch (lower variable cost coal power would be replaced by much higher cost LNG power) in order to utilize the full amount of LNG to be contracted. This adversely affects the economic viability of the project and would place a heavy financial burden on MSEB; and (b) the project is not part of the least-cost sequence for Maharashtra power development. Local coal and gas are the preferred choices for base load power generation...
>
> [I]t would appear worthwhile for you to explore possible ways to sustain their interest in investing in India's energy sector, in particular to see

whether it would be economically feasible to reshape the project to serve higher value intermediate loads in the Western Region.[266]

Enron was undeterred by the World Bank's refusal to fund the project or negative reports appearing in the Indian media. Consequently, Joseph Sutton, in a letter to Ajit Nimbalkar, wrote that Enron would hire a public-relations firm to "manage the media from here on." Sutton continued:

The project has solid support from all other agencies in Washington. We'll get there![267]

Weathering further lobbying by the government of India and Enron, the World Bank steadfastly refused to fund the project.[268] Facing a $635-million budget shortfall for the $920- million project, the company turned to the U.S. government and a consortium of private investors.[269] While a group of private foreign investors, led by the Bank of America and ABN Amro, provided approximately $150 million, and another group of Indian banks, led by the Industrial Development Bank of India, provided $95 million, political risk insurance and loan guarantees came from the U.S. government's Overseas Private Investment Corporation (OPIC) and Export-Import Bank (Ex-Im Bank)—institutions financed by U.S. taxpayers. OPIC contributed approximately $100 million in political risk insurance, and the Ex-Im Bank extended a loan guarantee of approximately $290 million in late 1994.[270] A State Department

---

[266] Letter from Heinz Vergin, World Bank country director for India, to Montek Singh Ahluwalia, secretary of economic affairs, Indian Ministry of Finance, April 30, 1993. Letter on file at Human Rights Watch.

[267] Letter from Joseph Sutton, chief operating officer of Enron, to Ajit Nimbalkar, chairman, Maharashtra State Electricity Board, June 23, 1993. Letter on file at Human Rights Watch.

[268] Letter from Heinz Vergin, World Bank country director for India, to R. Vasudevan, secretary for the Indian Ministry of Power, July 26, 1993. Letter on file at Human Rights Watch.

[269] The lead lawyer who represented the governmental financing agencies, the private international financial institutions, and the Indian financial institutions of Phase I of the Dabhol Power Project was Ellen W. Smith, counsel at the New York-based law firm White & Case.

[270] "Enron Power Project Secures $635 Million in Financing," *Economist Intelligence Unit*, April 19, 1995.

official, commenting on Enron's lobbying for U.S. government financing, told Human Rights Watch:

> Enron is a pain, they constantly lobby for OPIC and Ex-Im. They always make a case that their projects are very important for U.S. interests, who their international competitors are, and how many U.S. jobs their project will provide. They are aggressive and really work the government.[271]

The U.S. Government

On June 16, 1998, the secretary of state for the United States government, Madeleine Albright, outlined the goals of United States foreign policy, in a speech to the Senate Appropriations Committee: "We all agree that the United States is, and should remain, vigilant in protecting its interests, careful and reliable in its commitments and a forceful advocate for freedom, human rights, open markets and the rule of law."[272]

In the case of the Dabhol Power project, it seems that the government of the United States acted as a forceful advocate for open markets at the expense of human rights and the rule of law. Throughout the development and implementation of the Dabhol project, U.S. government officials and various governmental agencies including the Department of Energy, Department of State, Department of Commerce, and Central Intelligence Agency consistently lobbied

---

[271] Human Rights Watch interview with David Kirsch, Office of Economic Analysis, Department of State, Washington, D.C., June 18, 1998.

[272] United States Secretary of State Madeleine K. Albright, Opening Remarks Before the Senate Appropriations Committee, Subcommittee on Foreign Operations, Washington, D.C., June 16, 1998.

the Indian government heavily on behalf of the companies.[273] According to a 1995 article in the *New York Times*:

> [T]he negotiators for the Enron Corporation, the lead bidder in an American consortium, have been shadowed and assisted by a startling array of Government agencies. In a carefully-planned assault, the State and Energy Departments pressed the firms' [Enron, General Electric, and Bechtel] case. The American ambassador to India, Frank G. Wisner, constantly cajoled Indian officials. The Secretary of Energy, Hazel O'Leary, brought in delegations of other executives...to make the point that more American investment is in the wings if the conditions are right.
>
> To sweeten the pot, the Export-Import Bank of the United States and the Overseas Private Investment Corporation put together $400 million in financing. And working just behind the scenes, as it often does these

---

[273] This is not the only instance of concerted U.S. government lobbying for Enron. In 1995, according to the *Houston Chronicle*, U.S. officials lobbied the government of Mozambique to award Enron a $500-million contract to develop the Pande natural gas field. The company's primary competitor was Sasol, a South African firm. John Kachamila, then Mozambique's minister of mineral resources, told the *Houston Chronicle*: "There were outright threats to withhold development funds if we didn't sign, and sign soon. Their diplomats, especially Mike McKinley [deputy chief of the U.S. Embassy], pressured me to sign a deal that was not good for Mozambique. He was not a neutral diplomat. It was as if he was working for Enron. We got calls from American senators threatening us with this and that if we didn't sign. Anthony Lake [U.S. national security adviser] even called to tell us to sign... They put together a smear campaign against us... Enron was forever playing games with us and the embassy forever threatening to withdraw aid. Everyone was saying that we would not sign the deal because I wanted a percentage, when all I wanted was a better deal for the state... So Enron caved in to our demands, especially after the World Bank commissioned a study that found many of our concerns were warranted. Now let me ask you: Who is corrupt here? To me it is Enron for trying to shove this rotten deal down our throats." In the same article, the *Chronicle* quoted an unnamed State Department official saying, "This project represents tax revenue, hard currency earnings in a big way for the Mozambican state... If the Mozambicans think they can kill this deal and we will keep dumping money into this place, they should think again." At the time, $1.1 billion of the government of Mozambique's $1.5-billion budget was financed through foreign aid, at least $40 million from the United States Agency for International Development alone. See: John Fleming, "U.S. Foreign Aid was Lever that Moved Enron Deal," *Houston Chronicle*, November 1, 1995.

days, was the Central Intelligence Agency, assessing the risks of the project and scoping out the competitive strategies of Britain and other countries that want a big chunk of Indian market.[274]

The lobbying effort extended to the point of cautioning the Indian government to allow the project or face the consequences. For example, when the agreement was suspended by the newly elected Shiv Sena-BJP government in 1995, the U.S. Department of Energy issued a very strong statement threatening that the project's cancellation would seriously jeopardize U.S.-India relations and India's ability to attract foreign investment:

> We strongly support the reform process in India and believe that bringing private power is central to Indian economic development. The counter-guarantees that the Indian government has committed to provide for the first "fast-track" projects are essential to move those projects forward and establish a strong track record with international investors. While we recognize the need to limit the number of such guarantees, it will take time to bring alternative financing packages to market.
>
> The first of these power projects, Enron's Dabhol Project, has already reached financial closure and is under construction, sending a positive signal to international investors about the future of the Indian market. Failure to honor the agreements between the project partners and the various Indian governments will jeopardize not only the Dabhol Project but also the other private power projects being proposed for international financing.[275]

The statement was so strong that other U.S. officials, namely Amb. Frank Wisner, had to reassure officials of the Indian government that the U.S. Energy Department did not have the authority to cancel or block foreign investment in India. Instead, Wisner argued that the intent of the statement was to advise India that cancellation of the project would make it more difficult to attract foreign

---

[274] David E. Sanger, "How Washington Inc. Makes a Sale," *New York Times*, February 19, 1995.
[275] "Statement on the Cancellation of the Dabhol Power Project," United States Department of Energy, June 5, 1995.

investment.[276] Wisner's support for the company and the project was steadfast. According to the *Far Eastern Economic Review*:

> Enron found a powerful ally in the U.S. government. Ambassador Frank Wisner took up Enron's cause and hammered home to Indian officials that the two countries' newly established business ties would suffer if the Dabhol project were canceled altogether. The backing of Wisner..."speaks volumes for Enron's ability to rope powerful people in to help their cause," says a top official in the Power Ministry who was with the Power Ministry when the Dabhol deal was initially cleared. "The Indian government was clearly intimidated by Enron's clout."[277]

Commenting on his role, Wisner told Human Rights Watch, "I did say that cancellation of the deal could jeopardize foreign investment in the country. There were many statements about the project at the time, I was the ambassador and authorized all of them and stand behind every one of them."[278]

Given the stated goals of U.S. foreign policy, the fact that this is a project of U.S. companies, and the Overseas Private Investment Corporation (OPIC) and the Ex-Im Bank have labor rights and human rights conditionalities placed on their financing, respectively, it would be reasonable to assume that equal concern would be accorded to human rights. This was not the case, however.

The Overseas Private Investment Corporation is required to address labor rights in the course of its lending. OPIC contractually binds recipients of its financing to respect labor rights in the course of their operations. These activities are monitored by OPIC and reported on internally.[279] Of greater relevance in the

---

[276] "Enron Power-Moves Afoot to Take Heat Out of Dabhol Row," Reuters, June 26, 1995.

[277] "Alive and Well..."

[278] Human Rights Watch telephone interview with former United States Ambassador to India Frank Wisner; New York, July 16, 1998. Other governments would follow suit. The former chancellor of the exchequer for the government of the United Kingdom, Kenneth Clarke, would issue similar statements while leading a trade delegation to India. See: Clarence Fernandez, "U.S., Britain Warn India Over Enron Deal," Reuters, June 5, 1995.

[279] According to the OPIC Policy Handbook: **Other Requirements:** OPIC is prohibited by statute from supporting projects that contribute to violations of internationally recognized worker rights. OPIC insurance and finance agreements require the investor to agree to respect these rights, including the rights of association, collective bargaining and acceptable working conditions with respect to wages, hours of work, occupational health and safety and minimum age requirements. **Monitoring & Compliance:** OPIC

case of the Dabhol Power Corporation, the Ex-Im Bank is required to consider human rights broadly in its financing packages. Provisions in the Ex-Im Bank policies address general human rights issues, such as arbitrary detention, torture, freedom of expression, and freedom of association. But the policy is weak and grudging: Ex-Im Bank's policy manual avers, for example, that "there is no internationally accepted definition of what constitutes human rights," thus ignoring the extensive legal and monitoring framework achieved by the United Nations. The Ex-Im Bank can "deny its financing for human rights reasons only if the President [of the U.S.] through authority delegated to the Secretary of State, determines that such a denial would be in the national interest."[280] Otherwise, according to the bank's policy, "Ex-Im Bank should not deny applications for nonfinancial or noncommercial reasons." [281]

However, on every Ex-Im Bank transaction exceeding $10 million, the State Department is required to conduct a human rights impact assessment "to determine if it may give rise to significant human rights concerns." This review examines "both the general status of human rights and the effect of the export on human

---

systematically monitors investor compliance with U.S. economic, environmental, worker rights and corrupt practices representations through questionnaires, investor reporting and site visits. Noncompliance may constitute a default under OPIC insurance contracts and loan agreements.

[280] From Section 24 of the Policy Manual of the Export Import Bank of the United States. The relevant sections of the human rights policy are as follows—**Definition**: Human rights are basic protections to which a human being in a given country has a just claim. The United Nations Universal Declaration of Human Rights outlines very broad human rights principles, such as freedom of expression, religion, and assembly, and proscriptions against torture, discrimination and arbitrary arrest. However, there is no internationally accepted definition of what constitutes human rights. **Policy**: Ex-Im Bank can deny its financing for human rights reasons only if the President, through authority delegated to the Secretary of State, determines that such a denial would be in the national interest. A specific human rights review is conducted by the State Department for every transaction over $10·million to determine if it may give rise to significant human rights concerns. This review examines both the general status of human rights and the effect of the export on human rights in the importing country. **Rationale:** Section 2(b)(1)(B) of the Export-Import Bank Act of 1945, as amended, was amended in 1978 by P.L. 95-630, 92 Stat. 3724 (the Chafee Amendment). This amendment states that Ex-Im Bank should not deny applications for nonfinancial or noncommercial reasons (i.e., for policy reasons) unless the President of the United States determines that the denial is in the national interest. Interest areas on which a particular transaction may receive a denial include international terrorism, nuclear proliferation, environmental protection and human rights....

[281] Ibid.

rights in the importing country" and has been required since 1978.[282] Since Enron received between $290 and $300 million in U.S. government loan guarantees for the Dabhol Power project, the State Department was required to conduct a human rights impact assessment. The assessment was conducted by the U.S. Embassy in India, which provides the State Department with information on the human rights situation within the country.

As the ambassador and head of the U.S. Embassy in India, Mr. Wisner—in stark contrast to his role as advocate for Enron's commercial interests—was silent on the issue of human rights. When we asked former Ambassador Wisner about the human rights violations that took place in Maharashtra related to the Dabhol Power project in 1997, he responded:

> Look into the facts carefully about "protests." They were not protests—local villagers didn't like the amount of money they got from Enron in compensation and wanted to get more from the company. I do not know about the record of the Maharashtra police and don't know whether there were any human rights violations. I am not aware of what went down in the village, but they were probably exaggerated. I have never seen any information on human rights violations related to Dabhol and can't say anything about them. If you think there are human rights violations, you should go down to India and get the facts. If you want to know about human rights, talk to the Maharashtra Police. I don't know anything about the protests and suggest that you go to India and find out. Why do you want to talk to me?[283]

When we informed Mr. Wisner that we had investigated human rights violations in the area, he replied, "Well then, you have all the information you need. Why do you need to talk to me? I told you what I think of the project and my opinions."[284]

It is a matter of serious concern to Human Rights Watch that the former ambassador appears to have given no consideration to human rights violations in this context. It suggests a willingness on the part of the United States government to discount human rights when commercial interests are at stake. We believe that

---

[282] See footnote 280, on the human rights policies in the Policy Manual of the Export-Import Bank of the United States.

[283] Human Rights Watch telephone interview with former United States Ambassador to India Frank Wisner; New York, July 16, 1998.

[284] Ibid.

the ambassador had ample opportunity to look into the issue; and could with difficulty have missed references to it in the Indian press, made these determinations himself. For example, barely two days after the attack by Enron contractors in Kathalwadi village, and after several months of protests and police reprisals, Wisner visited the Dabhol Power project on April 3, 1997, accompanied by India's minister of power, S. Venugopalachari.[285] Many of the demonstrations were detailed in national newspapers, and a cursory consultation with NGOs would have exposed Wisner to the problem.

Frank Wisner was named to the board of directors of Enron Oil & Gas, a subsidiary of the Enron Corporation, on October 28, 1997, a few months after leaving his posting in India.[286]

Following admissions by representatives at the Ex-Im Bank that they were unaware of the human rights policies that applied to Ex-Im Bank lending, Human Rights Watch filed a Freedom of Information Act request to obtain all documents referring to the human rights review of the Dabhol Power Project. We received a confirmation of our request by the Ex-Im Bank, dated July 23, 1998.[287] Later, we received the impact assessment and a letter from the Ex-Im Bank In a letter dated October 1, 1998, informing us that there were no other documents concerning human rights in relation to the loan guarantee. The State Department's impact assessment itself is minimal. It states, in its entirety, "The State Department has no objection to this case on political grounds or on the basis of human rights issues."[288] The correspondence and impact assessment are reprinted in Appendix A.

A human rights impact assessment conducted in 1994-1995 could not have predicted violations in 1996-1998 But in 1993-1994, demonstrations and reprisals had already begun. Moreover, the complete lack of interest, as in the case of Mr. Wisner, the highest-ranking State Department official in India; the complete lack of knowledge, as in the case of the general counsel's office of the Ex-Im Bank; and the complete lack of information, as the impact assessment obtained from the Ex-

---

[285] *Dabhol Samvad...*, Vol. 1, No. 3, p. 4.

[286] "Enron Oil & Gas Company Elects Frank Wisner, Three New Enron Corporation Representatives to Board," Enron Corporation press release, October 28, 1998.

[287] Letter from the Export-Import Bank of the United States to Human Rights Watch, July 23, 1998.

[288] Letter from the Export-Import Bank of the United States, October 1, 1998. The attached impact assessment is undated and is not sourced, other than a handwritten note to Human Rights Watch stating, "From Export-Import Bank Board of Directors Memorandum." The written correspondence between Human Rights Watch and the Export-Import Bank is reprinted in Appendix A below.

Im Bank illustrates, demonstrate that human rights was not a consideration for the U.S. government. This apathy continues to have relevance now, as financing is arranged for Phase II of the project.

Phase II Financing

With an estimated cost of $1.5 billion and a capacity of 1,440 megawatts, Phase II of the project is slated to be almost twice the size of the $920-million, 740-megawatt Phase I.[289] Initially, the same actors, primarily the U.S. government's Export-Import Bank and OPIC as well as private investors, were expected to finance Phase II. Ex-Im Bank, for example, could have extended up to $500 million for the second phase of the project.[290] OPIC and Ex-Im Bank involvement, however, was suspended in May 1998 because of the underground nuclear tests that India and Pakistan had recently conducted: President Clinton imposed sanctions against India and Pakistan prohibiting the extension of all non-humanitarian aid and trade programs, including OPIC and Ex-Im Bank financing. Enron's response was that, "as a company doing business in India, we were not and we are not in favor of sanctions...."[291] The company predicted that sanctions would be lifted by the end of 1998.

The absence of OPIC and Ex-Im Bank financing created serious problems for Phase II planning. Publicly, Enron would not comment on the extent of the damage done by the loss of OPIC and Ex-Im Bank funding, stating only: "We are monitoring the situation and it is premature for us to predict any potential impact on our projects."[292] Later, the company would again reassure investors that sanctions would not affect the construction of Phase II of the Dabhol Power project.[293]

The business press and government officials were much more skeptical. *Platt's Commodity News*, a leading industry publication, reported that Enron's funding was in jeopardy because of the inability to access OPIC and Ex-Im Bank

---

[289] "Enron Seeking Power Plant Funding from Indian Financiers," *Platt's Commodity News*, June 28, 1998.

[290] "Japan's Sumitomo Asked to Lead India Power Plant Funding," *Platt's Commodity News*, July 20, 1998.

[291] "Sanctions Against India May be Lifted by Year-end—Enron," Press Trust of India, September 1, 1998.

[292] "Enron Assessing Impact of Sanctions on India," Reuters, May 14, 1998.

[293] "Enron Says Sanctions Won't Slow India Plant," Reuters, May 19, 1998.

financing.²⁹⁴ Equally telling was a State Department official's assessment in June 1998:

> Currently, Enron is in a lot of trouble. With the nuclear tests, OPIC and Ex-Im funding has been suspended. Enron is not as big as other oil companies and cannot finance projects of this size off their balance sheet, so they have to rely on financing like OPIC and Ex-Im. India is a big project and the lack of financing will hurt them.²⁹⁵

Enron scrambled to handle the setback, announcing on September 1, 1998 that it had secured $1 billion in financing from international commercial banks. The company obtained a $200 million loan guarantee from the Export-Import Bank of Belgium and $50 million from the Export-Import Bank of Japan (J-Exim) as part of the $1 billion financing package.²⁹⁶ The company also announced that $300 million would be obtained from Indian banks, led by the Indian government's Industrial Development Bank of India. The State Bank of India announced an "in principle" agreement to loan $150 million for Phase II of the project.²⁹⁷ On November 9, 1998, the Indian government's Industrial Finance Corporation provided an $83 million loan for Phase II.²⁹⁸ The State Bank of India and state-owned Industrial Development Finance Corporation announced their intent to loan $100 million for Phase II.²⁹⁹ The Indian government, however, did not extend a counter-guarantee for Phase II.³⁰⁰ Following the announcement that it had secured financing, the company said that it would begin construction of Phase II in the fourth quarter (October to December) of 2001.³⁰¹

None of the institutions that have agreed to finance Phase II have human rights conditionalities in general, or anything comparable to OPIC and Ex-Im

---

[294] "Enron India Power Plant Funding Threatened by Sanctions," *Platt's Commodity News*, May 13, 1998.

[295] Human Rights Watch interview with David Kirsch.

[296] "Enron Unit Secures Funds for India Power Plant," Reuters, September 1, 1998.

[297] "State Bank of India Approves Loan to Enron," Reuters, November 4, 1998.

[298] "India's IFC Extends $154 Mln in Loans to 2 Power Projects," Reuters, November 9, 1998.

[299] Sangita Mehta, "SBI, IDFC to Enter Takeout Deal for Dabhol," *Business Standard*, Bombay, November 12, 1998.

[300] "Enron Ties Up $US1 Billion for Phase 2 of Indian Project," Press Trust of India, September 1, 1998.

[301] "Enron Unit Secures Funds for India Power Plant," Reuters, September 1, 1998.

policies, to regulate their transactions. Nevertheless, Human Rights Watch considers that because of the abuses which occurred during the construction of Phase I and the existing prohibition on freedom of expression and peaceful assembly in Ratnagiri district, no financial institution can avoid responsibility for human rights violations if it finances Phase II without appropriate safeguards to protect human rights. Moreover, the consortium of public and private investors that financed Phase I—the Bank of America, ABN Amro, the consortium led by the Industrial Bank of India, OPIC, and Ex-Im Bank—bear special responsibility for the human rights violations because of a lack of due diligence which led to a failure to address and condemn the human rights violations while they extended financial support for this project.

On November 7, 1998, the U.S. government "eased" sanctions against India and reauthorized OPIC and Ex-Im Bank funding for projects in India, but at this writing it is unclear whether the company will try to secure U.S. government funding.[302]

---

[302] "U.S. Lifting of Sanctions, Boost to Infrastructure Projects Likely," *Business Line*, November 7, 1998.

IX. Conclusion

Since its inception in 1992, the Dabhol Power project has been at the center of controversy. Persistent allegations of corruption, lack of transparency, the reportedly high cost of electricity, and the project's detrimental impact on the environment and on peoples' livelihoods have all played a role in fostering opposition to the project at the international, national, state, and local levels. In 1994-95, as opposition parties, the Shiv Sena and BJP made the project and the aforementioned issues part of their campaign. Once the Shiv Sena-BJP coalition came to power, the government decided that its deal with Enron was acceptable, reversed its previous position and wholeheartedly supported the project—regardless of its own internal investigations or public opinion. Once the state government reversed its stance, people turned to the courts as a remedy for their grievances. The courts, however, did not address any of the controversial aspects of the project. Instead, as the CITU case illustrates, the judiciary would look the other way and dismiss claims rather than adjudicate or arbitrate a case where billions of dollars were at stake—even when faced with substantial evidence of irregularities during this project's development.

In this context, the demonstrations against the Dabhol Power project represent the last effort by individuals, who cannot match the financial and political influence of a transnational corporation like Enron, to voice their concerns and express their opposition to a project that has a profound impact on their lives. Although the vast majority of protests were peaceful and protected under international standards safeguarding freedom of expression and assembly, the state chose to silence dissent against the Dabhol Power project through arbitrary arrests, beatings, and targeted harassment of opposition leaders, rather than honestly or responsibly address their concerns. The perpetrators of these human rights violations must be investigated and punished.

The state government is not the only actor responsible for human rights violations. These abuses took place as a response to opposition to the Dabhol Power Corporation. In the oil and gas industry, corporations are often called on to respect human rights at the point where their operations and those of abusive forces intersect: when abusive forces are contracted to companies for security; when opposition to corporate activity is met with a repressive response by the state; or when the government refuses to respect human rights in order to give a corporation some advantage. In the case of the Dabhol Power project, all of these factors are in evidence: the Dabhol Power Corporation paid abusive state forces while they committed human rights violations against opponents of the company's project, and the company directly benefited from the human rights violations. The company's responsibility in these acts obligates it to publicly condemn human rights violations and to implement clear and meaningful policies ensuring that human rights violations do not take place as a result of its operations.

Similarly, the institutions that funded this project, namely the U.S. government and private financial institutions, were negligent because they failed to monitor the project for human rights violations while they extended hundreds of millions of dollars in support for it. The U.S. government has a special obligation to ensure respect for human rights because of its stated foreign policy objectives, its considerable lobbying on behalf of the project, and because it seemingly ignored its own regulatory requirements to assess the risk to human rights. As a financier of the project, it should investigate and audit its financing of the project to determine whether any public funds were used to finance illegal activities.

In a general sense, the human rights abuses that have occurred because of the Dabhol Power project underscore the need for all institutions involved—the companies, the home and host governments of the consortium, the public and private financing institutions—to implement binding regulations to ensure that the activities of transnational corporations do not foster human rights violations and to create institutional mechanisms to monitor the effect of investment on human rights.

The case of the Dabhol Power project raises another disturbing issue. Typically, abusive behavior by state forces on behalf of energy companies is believed to take place in relation to companies that, in partnership with highly abusive governments, operate in unstable environments; examples are the activities of British Petroleum in Colombia, Shell in Nigeria, or Unocal in Burma. Often, the argument used to defend doing business in such climates is that increased foreign investment is the best way to improve human rights.

The Dabhol Power project is not located in an unstable or conflicted area, nor is DPC a partner with a repressive government. India is the world's largest democracy, with a vigorous civil society, a general culture of human rights, legal protections, an active judiciary, and an acceptance of free expression and peaceful assembly. If increased investment necessarily leads to improvements in human rights and respect for the rule of law, then how can the human rights violations as a result of the Dabhol Power project be explained? The conflict that has taken place in Ratnagiri district, indeed, has flowed directly from the conduct of the DPC and the state. Opposition by villagers who saw their lands seized and their waters polluted and diverted also began with, and is attributable to, the requirements of the DPC project. The abuses visited upon dissenting villagers also are traceable to the supposedly beneficial investment by the parent-company of DPC, Enron.

Conclusion

The Dabhol Power project may teach a lesson to governments and companies who lobby for business and investment: Unless an explicit and programmatic commitment to human rights exists, respect and protection for these rights will not improve, and may deteriorate, even in countries that are considered democratic and open.

Appendix A: Correspondence Between Human Rights Watch and the Export-Import Bank of the United States

Correspondence Between Human Rights Watch and the Export-Import Bank of the United States

HUMAN RIGHTS WATCH
350 Fifth Avenue, 34th Floor
NY, NY 10118
Phone: 212-216-1251
Fax: 212-736-1300
E-mail: ganesaa@hrw.org
Website: http://www.hrw.org

Kenneth Roth
Executive Director
Michele Alexander
Development Director
Carroll Bogert
Communications Director
Reed Brody
Advocacy Director
Cynthia Brown
Program Director
Barbara Guglielmo
Finance & Administration Director
Susan Osnos
Associate Director
Wilder Tayler
General Counsel
Lotte Leicht
Brussels Office Director
Joanna Weschler
United Nations Representative

DIVISION DIRECTORS
Peter Takirambudde
Africa
José Miguel Vivanco
Americas
Sidney R. Jones
Asia
Holly Cartner
Europe and Central Asia
Hanny Megally
Middle East and North Africa
Joost R. Hiltermann
Arms
Lois Whitman
Children's Rights
Regan E. Ralph
Women's Rights

BOARD OF DIRECTORS
Jonathan Fanton
Chair
Robert L. Bernstein
Founding Chair
Lisa Anderson
William Carmichael
Dorothy Cullman
Gina Despres
Adrian W. DeWind
Irene Diamond
Fiona Druckenmiller
Edith Everett
Vartan Gregorian
Alice H. Henkin
Stephen L. Kass
Marina Pinto Kaufman
Bruce Klatsky
Harold Hongju Koh
Josh Mailman
Samuel K. Murumba
Andrew Nathan
Jane Olson
Peter Osnos
Kathleen Peratis
Bruce Rabb
Sigrid Rausing
Anita Roddick
Orville Schell
Sid Sheinberg
Gary G. Sick
Malcolm Smith
Domna Stanton
Maureen White
Maya Wiley

Mr. Howard Schweitzer
Office of the General Counsel
United States Export-Import Bank
811 Vermont Avenue, N.W.
Washington, D.C. 20571

July 16, 1998

Re: Freedom of Information Act Request

Dear Mr. Schweitzer,

Pursuant to our phone conversation, this is a written request under the Freedom of Information Act.

I request that a copy of documents containing the following information be provided to me:

Project and loan information for the $290-$300 million loan guarantee from the Export-Import Bank of the United States, provided for the Dabhol Power Corporation to construct a 695-740 Megawatt power project located in the state of Maharashtra in India. The financing was approved in 1994-1995. The Dabhol Power Corporation is a consortium comprised of three U.S. multinational corporations: Enron, General Electric, and Bechtel.

According to the policy Handbook of the Export-Import Bank, under Section 2(b)(1)(B) of the Export-Import Bank Act of 1945 (as amended), "a specific human rights review is conducted by the State Department for every transaction over $10 million to determine if it may give rise to significant human rights concerns. This review examines both the general status of human rights and the effect of the export on human rights in the importing country."

Any information or documents pertaining to the human rights review related to the financing and loan guarantee of the Dabhol Power Corporation by the Export-Import Bank of the United States.

In order to help determine my status to assess fees, you should know that I am a Researcher at Human Rights Watch, a not-for-profit, nongovernmental organization investigating issues related to human rights in India for the purposes of research and not for commercial use.

Thank you for consideration of my request.

Sincerely,

Arvind Ganesan
Researcher
Human Rights Watch
350 Fifth Avenue, 34th Floor
NY, NY 10118
Ph: 212-216-1251
Fax: 212-736-1300
E-mail: ganesaa@hrw.org

BRUSSELS   HONG KONG   LONDON   LOS ANGELES   MOSCOW   NEW YORK   RIO DE JANEIRO   WASHINGTON

EXPORT-IMPORT BANK
OF THE UNITED STATES

July 23, 1998

Arvind Ganesan
Human Rights Watch
350 Fifth Avenue, 34th Floor
New York, NY 10118

Re: FOIA Request # 19980083

Dear Mr. Ganesan:

This letter acknowledges receipt of your Freedom of Information Act (FOIA) request dated July 17, 1998. This request has been designated number 19980083.

The Export-Import Bank of the United States (Ex-Im Bank) intends to disclose the requested records concerning the Dabhol Power project to the fullest extent of the law. Ex-Im Bank records are dispersed throughout the agency and the United States. Please be assured that we are processing your request as expeditiously as possible. Staff workload and limited resources may delay completion. Please consider this as a notice that additional time may be required to process your request.

If you have any further questions, please contact the undersigned at (202) 565-3229. Thank you.

Sincerely,

H. A. Schweitzer

Howard A. Schweitzer
Counsel for Administration

811 VERMONT AVENUE, N.W. WASHINGTON, D.C. 20571

EXPORT-IMPORT BANK
OF THE UNITED STATES

October 1, 1998

Arvind Ganesan
Human Rights Watch
350 Fifth Avenue, 34th Flr
New York, NY 10118

Re: FOIA Request #19980083

Dear Mr. Ganesan:

This letter is in response to the above numbered Freedom of Information Act (FOIA) request regarding the State Department's human rights review of the Dabhol Power Project.

The Export-Import Bank is releasing all responsive records in their entirety. No other responsive records were located.

If you have any questions, please call Howard Schweitzer of our FOIA Office at (202) 565-3229. Thank you very much for your inquiry.

Sincerely,

Peter A. Barton
Assistant Chief Financial Officer

Enclosure

811 VERMONT AVENUE, N.W.   WASHINGTON, D.C. 20571

From Export-Import Bank Board of Directors Memorandum.

10

STATE DEPARTMENT COMMENTS

The State Department has no objection to this case on political grounds or on the basis of human rights issues.

not relevant to request

Appendix B: Report of the Cabinet Sub-Committee to Review the Dabhol Power Project

REPORT OF THE CABINET SUB-COMMITTEE TO REVIEW THE DABHOL POWER PROJECT

CHAPTER I

INTRODUCTION

1.1 In terms of the decision of the Cabinet of the Maharashtra Government, a Sub-Committee of the Cabinet was constituted on 3rd May 1995 (Annexure I) to review the Dabhol Power Project of the Dabhol Power Company (DPC), a private company with unlimited liability, promoted by the Enron Power Development Corporation, U.S.A. and to report whether it subserves the interests of the State of Maharashtra. The Sub-Committee was headed by Shri Gopinath Munde, Deputy Chief Minister and consisted of Shri Sudhir Joshi, Minister for Revenue, Shri Hashu Advani, Minister for Finance and Planning, and Shri Liladhar Dake, Minister for Industries, Cottage Industries Law & Judiciary as members. Shri Hashu Advani, Minister for Finance and Planning could not attend after the first meeting due to his ill-health.

1.2 The terms of reference of the Sub-Committee were as under:

(i) The reasons for not calling competitive bids.
(ii) Whether there was any secrecy in relation to the discussions and negotiations on the project.
(iii) Whether the capital cost of the project is reasonable.
(iv) Whether any unusual or undue concessions were given for the project.
(v) Whether the rate of purchase of power is reasonable.
(vi) Whether there will be any adverse impact on the environment in the Konkan area because of the project.
(vii) How far the project is useful for the development of the State, and
(viii) Any other important issues relating to the project.

1.3. As per the G.R. No. BPC 1095/CAR-2670/Energy II dated 3rd May 1995, Secretary (Energy) acted as coordinating Secretary and, along with Secretary (Finance), Principal Secretary (Planning), and Principal Secretary (Law and Judiciary), assisted the Sub-Committee in their deliberations.

1.4 The Sub-Committee met on the following dates in May 1995: 3rd, 9th, 10th, 16th, 17th, 18th, 19th, 25th, 26th, and 29th and heard the representatives of institutions and interested individuals. The Sub-Committee also heard the representatives of the DPC, who made oral and written presentations. The Chairman and other officers of the Maharashtra State Electricity Board (MSEB) were present on all the days when the Cabinet Sub-Committee met. Detailed oral and written presentations on several days were made by the Chairman and other officers of the MSEB on the background of the project, as well as on the various issues relating to the project. The other institutions and persons who made oral and/or written presentations before the Sub-Committee were:

Sr. No.	Name of the Institution	Person represented	Date of meeting
1.	Tata Institute of Social Sciences	Dr. Vidya Rao	9.5.95
2.	Prayas, Pune	Shri Subodh Wagle	18.5.95
3.	Soclean, Mumbai	Shri Debi Goenka	18.5.95
4.	Dev and Associates, Pune	Shri Jayant Deo	18.5.95
5.	Mumbai Grahak Panchayat	Shri Shirish Deshpande	18.5.95
6.	Swadeshi Jagan Manch	Shri Ravindru Mahajan	18.5.95
7.	Janata Dal	Smt. Mrinal Gore Shri P.B. Samant Shri P.D. Kunte	18.5.95
8.	Rambhau Mhalgi Prabodhini	Shri Kulkarni V.G.	18.5.95
9.	-	Shri K.S. Joshi	19.5.95
10.	Save Bombay Committee	Shri Kisan Mehta	19.5.95
11.	Independent Power Producers Association of India, Mumbai	Shri Harry Dhaul	19.5.95
12.	Enron Virodhi Sangharsh Samiti	Shri R.G. Karnik Shri A.D. Golandaj Shri Shankar Salvi	19.5.95
13.	-	Shri S.R. Paranjpe	19.5.95

Sr. No.	Name of the Institution	Person represented	Date of meeting
14.	Lal Nishan Paksha	Shri Raja Patwardhan	25.5.95
15.	Dabhol Power Corporation	Ms. Rebecca Mark and others	25.5.95 26.5.95
16.	Lok Vihyan Sanghatana, Pune	Dr. Sulbha Brahme	written submissions
17.	Tata Energy Research Centre	Dr. Pachauri	written submissions

1.5 A large volume of evidence was presented, running to several thousands of pages covering almost all aspects of the Dabhol project. The Committee procured the files and documents on Enron/DPC project maintained by the Energy Department of the Government of Maharashtra and also many other documents related to the deal.

1.6. At the outset, the Sub-Committee expresses its deep appreciation and gratitude, particularly to the voluntary agencies and individuals who had taken extraordinary pains to marshal critical facts about a complex project.

CIRCUMSTANCES LEADING TO THE REVIEW

1.7 The Dabhol Power Project of the Dabhol Power Company (DPC) promoted by the Enron Power Development Corporation—which for easy reference is referred to as the "Project"—had invited loud public criticism all over India, although the Project belongs only to Maharashtra. Cutting across all political and ideological differences, public men and women of acknowledged competence, integrity, and eminence had severely questioned the Project. The Project became the subject of techno-economic and political debate. Many environmentalists too joined the public outcry. The press, in general, became critical of the Project. The Project generated one of the most intense intellectual debates at the national level on any single commercial venture. But the issue was not confined to the press or seminars or intellectual debates. It soon took the shape of a mass agitation with the ordinary public getting involved in satyagraha, giving the Project law and order dimensions. Thus, during the years 1993 and 1994, the Project snowballed into a major public issue, particularly in Maharashtra where elections to the State Assembly were due in February 1995.

1.8 The public debate on the Enron Project served to highlight several intriguing, unusual, and unreasonable features of what was viewed by many as a thoroughly one-sided arrangement in favour of the DPC, and against the national interest, in particular, against the interests of Maharashtra. What the public perceived as secret and surreptitious was the manner in which the negotiations were conducted and the Project was approved. The intriguing conduct of the previous State Government only served to heighten the rising suspicion and apprehensions in the public mind that the previous government had a lot to conceal. The previous government had also claimed confidentiality about the Project papers which only added to the public apprehension that there were extraneous motives and corrupt elements in this Project. Even when some public spirited persons challenged the Project in the Court of Law, the previous government insisted before the Court that it shall not make the crucial documents of the Project public.

1.9 As it happens, and it is bound to happen in all democracies, the widely suspected and highly questioned Project became an issue in the State Assembly elections held in January 1995. The Shiv Sena-BJP alliance which fought the elections against the then ruling Congress had emphatically declared in their joint electoral declaration addressed to the electorate of Maharashtra that if they came to power, the Project would be reviewed and if it was found to be against the interests of the country, the State of Maharashtra, and the people, it would be canceled. The Joint Manifesto of the Shiv Sena-BJP alliance for the Maharashtra Assembly Elections-1995 had made a commitment that the "Suspicious Enron deal will be reviewed." Thus, the Enron issue had become a trans-party and trans-political public and electoral issue involving the entire public of Maharashtra where the State elections were held early this year. Though the polling in a majority of the constituencies in the State elections concluded on 12th February 1995, the votes were counted much later in March, 1995 because of the staggered election programme in different States. The electoral verdict of the people of Maharashtra was in favour of the Shiv Sena-BJP alliance which assumed office on 14th March 1995 under the chief ministership of Shri Manohar Joshi. Thus, the Shiv Sena-BJP alliance had not merely secured the mandate of the people to review the Project, but under the mandate of the people, it was obliged to review the Project forthwith and in an expeditious manner, so as to restore the peoples' confidence in the institution of the government. It was in these circumstances that the new government appointed the present Sub-Committee to review and make recommendations on the Enron Project.

CHAPTER II

THE PROJECT IN BRIEF

2.1 The Project is being set up by DPC which is promoted by EPC of the U.S.A. in association with General Electric and Bechtel Engineering, also of U.S.A. The Project envisages two phases of implementation for establishing a total capacity of 2,015 MW at Dabhol on a Build Own and Operate basis (BOO) for which a Power Purchase Agreement (PPA) was signed having a duration of 20 years. MSEB has the option to extend the PPA by 5 or 10 years. If it does not do so, the PPA will terminate on its expiry date and MSEB can require that the power station be transferred at a price equal to 50 percent of the depreciated replacement cost. Phase I of the project involves installation of 695 MW capacity, the balance 1,320 MW being installed in Phase II. The Project is based entirely on imported fuel and Phase I would use imported distillate oil. After the installation of Phase II, the entire 2,015 MW capacity will be operated on imported Liquefied Natural Gas (LNG). The Enron Project is the first and only project in India solely based on imported LNG. The annual foreign exchange outgo at the current rupee-dollar rate is estimated at $1.45 billion which has a built in potential for increase on account of escalation. Phase I of the Project is to be commissioned in December 1997. The total cost of the Project is over $2.8 billion for both Phases, of which $910 million relates to Phase I. The arrangement between DPC and MSEB embodied in the PPA involves a guaranteed purchase of power at 90 percent PLF [Plant Load Factor] of the Project at rates calculated by a formula in the PPA which has built in escalation provisions. In addition, the Maharashtra Government has guaranteed payment of dues under the PPA by MSEB to DPC. This is also counter-guaranteed by the Central Government. The choice of Enron for the Project was made not by inviting public bids, but by private negotiations with a single party. Several features and provisions of the agreement between Enron and MSEB were intriguing and unusual and such intriguing features began to surface in public through the media and through <u>social</u> and <u>political</u> <u>activists.</u> The choice of Enron without inviting bids was challenged before the Courts. The previous administration had contended before the Courts that choice without bids was not improper. The Court held that the government could, in appropriate cases, make a choice without public bids. Even the judicial verdict did not allay the apprehensions of the public and the issue continued to rise like a tornado as exposure after exposure of the deal began to add to the unusual character of the Enron-MSEB arrangement. The several unusual, intriguing, and incredible aspects of the Enron-MSEB arrangement many of which were widely publicised and which led to public suspicion and apprehensions about the Project, were the starting point of the Sub-Committee's review work.

CIRCUMSTANCES LEADING TO THE SIGNING OF THE POWER PURCHASE AGREEMENT

2.2 The chronology of events clearly points out that the then State Government did not, at any stage, explore the possibility of getting competitive bids and preferred to deal with Enron alone in this matter. The chronology of events is as follows:

In June 1992: An Indian high-power delegation returns to India after a visit abroad in May/June 1992, during which Enron, it is claimed, showed interest to set up a power plant in India based on LNG technology.

On 10.06.92: Almost immediately, the Secretary (Power), Government of India, informed the MSEB Chairman at Delhi that a team of Enron officials would visit Maharashtra and requested him to show some sites on the coastline of Maharashtra so that the power plant could be set up there.

On 15.06.92: Within 5 days, the Enron team with representatives of General Electric, arrived in Delhi and had discussions with GOI officials.

On 17.06.92: Within the next two days, the Enron-GE officials arrived in Bombay.

On 18.06.92
& 19.06.92: They were taken to Ratnagiri, Pawas, Dabhol, and Nagothane. They were also shown Usar, Uran, and Nhava Sheva Port by helicopter.

On 19.06.92: A meeting of the team in MSEB's office was arranged with officials of the Maharashtra

	Government at which the team chose the Dabhol site.
On 20.06.92:	MoU [Memorandum of Understanding] between MSEB and Enron for the Dabhol project was signed.

2.3 Thus, in a matter of less than three days after its arrival in Bombay, an MoU was signed between Enron and MSEB in a matter involving a project of the value of over Rs. 10,000 crores at that time, with entirely imported equipment, in which, admittedly, no one in the Government had expertise or experience. In fact, the file does not even show what Enron was—what its history is, business or accomplishment. It looked more like an ad hoc decision rather than a considered decision on a durable arrangement with a party after obtaining adequate and reliable information. Neither the balance sheet and annual accounts of Enron, nor any information about its activities, area of operation, its associates, etc. was obtained by the government then or even later. Further, the MoU, as the then Secretary, Energy, Maharashtra Government has recorded, casts a responsibility on the MSEB to finalise certain decisions so that a proper Power Purchase Agreement could be signed "in sixty days." This MoU was termed as "one sided" by the World Bank in its letter dated 8th July, 1992. The CEA [Central Electricity Authority] had also considered it to be "one-sided" as referred in their comments contained in the enclosure to the letter dated 21st July 1992 from the Ministry of Power.

2.4 At the suggestion of then Secretary, Energy, Maharashtra and as approved by the then Chief Secretary and as repeatedly requested by the State Government, the Central Government secured the services of the World Bank to assess the Enron project. In fact, at one stage, Enron itself was seeking to involve the World Bank for finance and participation as, in the view of the then Chief Secretary, Maharashtra, "Enron is convinced that the World Bank has full and scientific knowledge of the working of the Power sector in India." This is despite the fact that the Finance Secretary felt that Enron would pre-empt the other projects of the State from getting World Bank assistance, if Enron were allowed access to the World Bank funds. However, later in its Report, the World Bank clearly advised that the Enron Project is (i) unviable, (ii) does not satisfy the test of least cost power, (iii) is too large and (iv) is not justified by the power demands of Maharashtra. Once the World Bank's assessment came and it clearly vetoed the Project, the response of all those who persistently asked for the World Bank advice, confessing that in those areas the Government did not have experience or expertise, was to underplay and even suppress it. Almost every official other than the then Secretary, Finance supported the Project ignoring the World Bank's advice. This report of the World Bank dated April 30, 1993 said that, as a project, in their view, it was unviable and they could not finance it. The efforts of the protagonists of the Enron deal were hence to regard World Bank's views as merely that of a consultant or, at best, of a financier of the Project. Its views were sought because the Government of Maharashtra had no expertise in the techno-commercial aspects of private power production at the international level. The World Bank's views covered all aspects including whether the Project would suit the interest of Maharashtra—and the World Bank advised that the Project as formulated did not suit the needs of MSEB. The World Bank's letter of April 30, 1993 is at Annexure II. The conclusion reached by the World Bank in para. 16 of the annexure to their letter was that, considering the data available regarding the Demand of Energy, "an LNG-based power plant operating in base load is not the least cost option for expanding power supply." It was also pointed out by the World Bank in para. 17 of the Annexure to their letter that, "the suggested load increase is unproven and the proposed high forecast is not a suitable basis for evaluating the Project." From the documents made available to the Sub-Committee and the presentation made before it, it is clear that neither any independent assessment of the demand of energy was made (though it was claimed that CEA has formed a group with MSEB representatives to study the demand for power), nor any comparative study of different fuels was carried out before opting for imported LNG as the fuel for the Project. In respect of these issues, MSEB merely pointed out the non-availability of local coal and gas and the environment-friendly nature of a LNG-based power plant as compared to a coal-based plant. The World Bank, in its further letter of 26.7.93 (which is at Annexure III) reconfirmed its earlier findings and advised the reshaping of the Enron Project to primarily serve higher value intermediate loads and stated that this would require consideration of a larger consumer base on a regional basis to share the risks and costs of the project. It also advised on the phasing and timing of the LNG project. The World Bank never certified the Project as viable at any point of time.

2.5 The chronology of events about the splitting of the capacity of the Project are as below:

20.06.92: The MoU was signed assuming a nominal capacity of 2,000 to 2,400 MW.

8.07.92: The World Bank team was available in Bombay for preparation of Request for Proposal (RFP) for the Nagothane Power Project. The team was requested to evaluate the MoU of Enron. The preliminary analysis, forwarded by the World Bank to the Government of Maharashtra via their letter of 8th July 1992, mentioned the one-sided nature of the MoU.

18.08.92: In the High Power Board meeting of the Government of India Secretaries held on 18.08.92, MSEB indicated that it had suggested that Enron may study the possibility of developing the project in two phases of 1,200 MW each. However, Enron was of the view that due to economies of scale, they would like to retain the configuration they had proposed.

29.08.92: Enron submitted an application to Chairman, FIPB [Foreign Investment Promotion Board] for a combined-cycle 2,550 MW power project based on LNG. It was envisaged that No. 2 fuel oil could be used to fuel the power station for up to one year following the commencement of commercial operation, depending on the availability of externally-sourced LNG. Initial generation of power was expected to begin in December, 1995. The power generation system would be initially using fuel oil and subsequently using LNG. The main plant equipment remain the same for No. 2 fuel and for LNG.

5.12.92: In the FIPB meeting of 5th December, 1992, Enron were informed that their proposal may be down-sized to enable it to be handled at the present stage. Two options were available: (a) scaling-down to 1,920 MW at a cost of U.S.$ 2.65 billion and (b) a project of 1,200 MW at a cost of U.S.$ 1.95 billion. It was brought out by Enron that if the size of the project came down to 1,200 MW, one train load of LNG would still have to be purchased and the surplus of gas marketed directly to industrial consumers. In view of the matching of one train load of LNG with the plant size of 1,920 MW, Enron agreed to work on the basis of 1,920 MW with the possibility of further expansion later.

3.02.93: FIPB approved the proposal to set up a 1,920 MW power plant (which capacity may be expanded to 2,550 MW at a future date) based on imported LNG.

12.03.93: Director, (Fund Bank), Ministry of Finance, Department of Economic Affairs, New Delhi informed the World Bank that the clearance to 1,920 MW Combined Cycle Gas Turbine project at Dabhol is given by the Government of India and requested the World Bank to consider this project for World Bank financing and requested the views of the World Bank on the DPC.

30.04.03: World Bank communicated their views on the DPC to Secretary, Department of Economic Affairs, Ministry of Finance, New Delhi.

The above chronology of events indicates that it is difficult to appreciate when and why the decision to split the project and to use No. 2 fuel oil for Phase I was taken. Nor is it clear that this was done after a careful consideration of the requirements of MSEB and the State of Maharashtra. In fact, it seems to address only the concerns of Enron. The conduct of the negotiations shows that the sole objective was to see that Enron was not displeased—it is as if Enron was doing a favour by this deal to India and to Maharashtra. In fact, the entire negotiation with Enron is an illustration of how not to negotiate, how not to take a weak position in negotiations, and how not to leave the initiative to the other side.

CHAPTER III

3.1 The Cabinet Sub-Committee has carefully considered the various documents presented to it as also those obtained by it and the various points submitted during the oral presentations by the different institutions/persons who appeared before it. The Sub-Committee also received a copy of the statement of Shri Sharad Pawar, Leader of the Opposition in the Council. The response of the Sub-Committee on some of the major points raised by him is given in Annexure IV. The findings of the Committee on the terms of reference are given below:

3.2 Reason for not having competitive bids:

The issue about competitive bidding has repeatedly arisen in the context of private sector power projects. The issue has now been settled by the new Government of India policy. The Lok Sabha Standing Committee on Energy (May 1995) in its 26th Report also deals with how the private negotiation policy was wrong. But between private negotiations between a single party and the Government, on the one hand, and competitive bidding as per the new policy, a third option also existed. In the third option, which is not as transparent as the second option—we involve more than one party in the negotiation for awarding the contract. The policy of competitive bidding was itself followed by the State of Maharashtra in respect of private power projects, as in the cases of Nagothane and Khaparkheda projects. There is no reason cited in any file note or correspondence as to why another bidding party could not have been involved in the Project. Involving another party does not make it an open bid, but prevents it from being a secret pact between the State and a chosen party. In fact, during the first visit of Enron on 18/19 June 1992, the team was shown, in addition to Dabhol, Nagothane and Ratnagiri, but they chose Dabhol. By not exploring the possibility of inviting another party capable of setting up such a project, the State Government deprived itself of the advantage of competitive bidding in the evaluation of the Project. It is this one-to-one dealing with Enron and absence of competition that led to secrecy and lack of transparency in the negotiation and handling of this Rs. 10,000 crore contract. As a result of this, the State Government could not resist successfully the insistence of Enron on confidentiality of negotiations for commercial or other reasons and ultimately this resulted in an uneven agreement. The Sub-Committee is aware that matters relating to lack of competitive bidding and secrecy in negotiations have been agitated before the High Court. While the High Court has said that the course followed by the State Government is not illegal or arbitrary, this does not mean that this is the best method, especially in respect of transactions involving public money where transparency is by far the most important criterion so as to bring credibility in Government functioning.

There was no effort on the part of the then Government to explore the possibility of involving another party interested in making private investment in the new power policy in India out of a number of multinational parties contacted by the Government during their visit abroad to market the power sector in India. The Sub-Committee has, therefore, no hesitation in concluding that this basic failure of the State Government that led to further problems in the one-to-one negotiations.

3.3 Whether there was any secrecy in relation to the discussions and negotiation in the Project:

The matter regarding secrecy in respect of Government's/MSEB's agreement with DPC was agitated in various High Court cases. It was alleged that the deal was shrouded in secrecy. It was also the contention of Government/MSEB that the proposal was deliberated at length for one-and-a-half years. The draft agreements were prepared from time to time and it was ultimately after 8 or 9 drafts that the PPA was finalised. It was, therefore, claimed that nothing was done secretly. The then Government/MSEB claimed confidentiality of documents on account of the commercial nature of the transactions. No doubt, the documents were shown to the parties to the litigation but this was done only on the instruction of the High Court. The Government refused to make these public nor were they made freely available to the Members of the Legislature. As soon as the present Government came to power, it demanded that the documents, PPA and Fuel Management Agreement should be made public and the DPC readily agreed to make it public. Therefore, it is very clear that even if the previous Government had not insisted on such great secrecy, there would not have been any adverse commercial impact, as claimed. Considering all these developments, the Sub-Committee concludes that while the principle of confidentiality of commercial transaction may be a sound principle in respect of private transactions, in the case of Government transactions where public finance is involved, recourse to such a method is always fraught with danger, raising suspicion in the minds of the people, regarding purity of the deal and, therefore, it was not correct on the part of the State Government to deprive general public access to the vital documents like the PPA and the Fuel Management Agreement.

The Sub-Committee has also noted the testimony given by Ms. Linda Powers, Vice President, Global Finance of Enron Development Corporation before a Committee of the U.S. House of Representatives, stating that, "...our company spent an enormous amount of its own money—approximately $20 million on this education and project development alone, not including any project costs." The Sub-Committee feels that these remarks need further clarification.

3.4 Whether the capital cost of the project is reasonable

The most intriguing aspect of the Enron project has been the incredibly high capital cost of the Rs. 4.49 crores per MW. The previous Government and Enron have been justifying it on the basis that it compares well with the capital cost of the other Fast Track Projects cleared for the private sector. The comparative table of the capital cost of the seven Fast Track Projects is as under:

Project	Capacity (Megawatts)	Type of Fuel	Cost per Megawatt (Rupees in Crores)
Enron	2,015	Gas (LNG)	4.49
Jagrupadu	235	Gas	3.52
Godavari	208	Gas	3.60
Vishakapatnam	1,000	Coal	5.81
Mangalore	1,000	Coal	5.08
Ib Valley	420	Coal	4.82
Zero unit NLC	250	Lignite	4.50

It is evident from the above data that the cost of the Enron Project is more comparable to the coal based projects than to gas based projects. Even as compared to the other gas based projects the cost of the DPC Project is clearly higher by at least 25 percent. Considering the fact that the other gas based projects, Jagrupadu and Godavari, are insignificant in capacity as compared to Enron, a comparison with them will be misleading. Being small projects, their capital cost per megawatt is bound to be higher. Even then, the capital cost of the Enron project is higher than the cost per megawatt of these smaller projects.

Capital cost of any project depends on the type of fuel used. Empirical evidence shows that the capital cost of coal-based power plants will be much higher than that of gas-based power plants.

The Committee had the opportunity to peruse the study on comparative capital costs of coal- and gas-based power plants conducted by the U.S.-based

Advanced Light Water Reactor Programme (ALWR, PALO ALTO, U.S.A.). The draft report is attached at Annexure V. If the findings of this report are applied to the present case, it would be clear that the capital cost of the DPC is on the high side and needs to be considerably reduced. The capital cost of the Enron Project which is gas-based cannot be compared with the capital cost of coal-based plants which could be 120-150 percent higher depending upon the type of coal used and also whether it is a combined cycle coal-based plant or not.

In fact the high capital cost wiped out the main advantage that the Dabhol power was supposed to bring. Because gas based technology was to be used, the capital cost of the Project should have been much cheaper than a coal based plant, whereas the running cost would have been higher. In the instant case we have lost the advantage of a lower capital cost from a gas based plant while still retaining the disadvantages of a higher running cost.

The Committee also had an opportunity to see the capital cost figures of projects implemented by Enron in other countries. It is clear that this is the costliest project being implemented by this company. The Committee noted that in one case at least, the difference in price was as high as 50 percent.

The 26th report of the Standing Committee on Energy (10th Lok Sabha) entitled "New Policy Initiatives in the Power Sector—Status of Their Implementation and Their Impact on the Economy" presented on 31.05.95, has also noticed that the cost of the Project was high as compared to the other gas-based projects and as compared to the cost of BHEL [Bharat Heavy Electricals Limited] turnkey offers. The report says:

> There are four gas-based and three coal based power projects in the private sector cleared by CEA so far. Out of the four gas-based projects, the per megawatt (MW) cost in respect of three projects (Jagrupadu, Godavari, and Puguthan) was between Rs. 3.52 crores and Rs. 3.74 crores while for Dabhol, the cost per MW was Rs. 4.19 crores. Of the three coal-based projects, the cost per MW of Vishakapatnam project at Rs. 5.82 crores is considerably higher than the Ib Valley at Rs. 4.82 crores and Mangalore project at Rs. 5.08 crores. BHEL in this connection has pointed out that turnkey costs in respect of projects with BHEL equipment could cost only around Rs. 3.6 crores to 4.3 crores per MW after making suitable adjustments for development cost, inflation and interest during construction. The cost per MW of power projects in general and Dabhol and Vishakapatnam projects in particular appear to be much higher than that indicated by BHEL. The Committee feel that guaranteed rate of return are tempting the investors to inflate their cost

to ensure better returns. According to experts, lack of competitive bidding has led to significant padding in the investment cost. The Committee desires that the Government should ensure that cost of private power projects should be so determined as it conforms to the simple tariff structure recommended in the preceding paragraph. Efforts should also be made to dispel doubts with regard to reasonableness of the cost of power projects.

The concluding remark—that effort should be made to dispel the doubts—is very important. In fact, the Standing Committee [Parliamentary Standing Committe on Energy] has mentioned on page 151 that the private investors appear to have a tendency to inflate costs which would finally lead to higher unit tariffs where the tariff structure is based on the cost-plus approach. In a project like this where escalations have been built in and a guaranteed 90 percent offtake of power is assured, the incentive to inflate costs could well be imagined.

3.5 Whether any unusual or undue concessions were given for the Project:

The Sub-Committee noted that in view of the assured returns to the Project, good profits are virtually guaranteed. This being so, the value of DPC shares] is likely to rise very rapidly. It will be quite easy for DPC to offer these shares at a very high premium to the Indian public. A good deal of this premium is due to the assured return guaranteed by the Government and to what can at best be described as a one-sided agreement. If elementary precautions to safeguard the interest of the State had been taken while negotiating the PPA, a clause could have been definitely inserted to the effect that the DPC would give Government of Maharashtra/MSEB the first option to purchase at par any share that they wish to offer in the Indian market. On the contrary, the clause regarding definition in the PPA clearly defines "change in ownership" in such a manner as to allow purchase of shares for a consideration payable in rupees out of the proceeds of the sale of a foreign currency which will enable foreign financial institutions and NRIs [Non-resident Indians] to buy shares without MSEB's consent.

The Sub-Committee has noted that a very high IRR [rate-of-return] of 25 percent has been conceded to this Project. Such a high rate of return is justifiable in cases where a scheme of incentives can help push up the PLF, as in coal plants. Coal plants normally operate at a lower PLF and a scheme of incentives based on a sliding scale of PLF can help to act as an incentive to the operator. However, in gas-based plants, as the technology itself is such that it normally operates at a PLF which is in the range of 90 percent, a higher IRR does not serve the purpose of an incentive for the operator to achieve a higher PLF. The Sub-Committee feels that the high IRR has not achieved the purpose of raising the PLF, but has only further bloated the profitability of DPC.

The above are some of the unusual features noticed by the Sub-Committee. Certain other unusual features have also been mentioned under the other issues examined in the report.

3.6 Whether the rate of purchase of power is unreasonable:

An impression has been created in the public mind that in 1997, Dabhol Power will cost only Rs. 2.40 per unit. Even if MSEB purchases power at Rs. 2.40, line losses, distribution costs, and other overheads will have to be added to this cost. The Sub-Committee estimates that the final cost to the consumers of Dabhol Power will be considerable higher.

The most amazing aspect of the entire Project is the fact that the tariff for power has been denominated in U.S. dollars. This means that, regardless of the fluctuations in the dollar-rupee exchange rate, the Project will always earn the same amount. In other words, they are permanently insulated from the vagaries of exchange-rate fluctuations. The Sub-Committee can see no reason whatsoever for this. Foreign direct investment (FDI) comes into this country in several different sectors. There is no restriction on the repatriation of profits legitimately earned by such investments. In no other case, however, is the entrepreneur protected against fluctuations in the international currency market. The Committee fails to see any reason why such preferential treatment should have been given to the power sector and to the DPC.

These unusual concessions makes the calculation of the exact amount that will be paid to MSEB to DPC virtually impossible. As it is the rate for power will depend on the cost of fuel, the contract and price of which is still indeterminate and has yet to be tied up. In addition, the price will
be affected by variations in the exchange rate. The entire exercise puts an impossible burden on the MSEB, and, therefore, on the consumers in Maharashtra. If the cost of the fuel and the rupee-dollar exchange rate rise (and there is no reason to suppose they will not) the effect will be to reduce and eliminate the competitive edge that Maharashtra now enjoys in the country.

The Sub-Committee also would like to point out that the popular impression that Dabhol Power will cost the consumers only Rs. 2.40 per unit is wrong for other reasons as well. Calculation shows that the raw cost of power at best bar is only 54 percent of the total cost to the consumer. The remaining 46 percent is accounted for by overheads, interest, depreciation and return on capital employed. Thus, to the figure of Rs. 2.40 per unit, we will have to add a further 46 percent in order to arrive at the price to be paid by the consumer. This is not all. In order to evacuate the power from Dabhol, MSEB will have to put up high tension lines at a capital cost of about Rs. 370 crores. The interest on the capital cost of these high tension lines to be provided by MSEB for evacuating the power from Dabhol will have to be added to the cost.

MSEB will also have to pay DPC for power supply within twenty-five days. The Committee notes that MSEB today has receivables of nearly 130 days. This means that while MSEB itself will not be able to collect its dues before four months, they will be paying DPC in less than one month. The working capital cost for MSEB will, therefore, rise considerably as a result. When all these things are taken into account, there is little doubt that instead of a figure of Rs. 2.40 per unit, the consumer will have to pay close to Rs. 3.50 per unit for Dabhol Power. In view of the above, the Sub-Committee concludes that the determination of tariff for power in U.S. dollars is a very unusual feature of the agreement and other features mentioned above, the consumer will have to pay a higher price for power than is justified.

3.7 Whether there will be any adverse impact on the environment in the Konkan area because of the Project:

The issue regarding environment got bogged down to whether LNG is an environment-friendly fuel or not as compared to coal. On this comparison—and this the only fuel (coal) which was compared with LNG and in no other respect as in every other respect coal had techno-commercial superiority in India—an impression was assiduously created that LNG, being an environment-friendly material, the environmental considerations are satisfied. The issue is not whether coal or gas is more environment-friendly. If the arguments used for Dabhol were considered as final, coal could never compete with LNG. So the environmental issue which was almost reduced to Coal vs. LNG argument, has not been properly appreciated.

The real environmental issue involved in the Dabhol Project is whether, environmentally, the location of Dabhol, which is in the Konkan (virtually the unpolluted part of Maharashtra) is proper or should the location have been elsewhere where industries have already been established or any other place which cannot boast of the green effects of the Konkan. Therefore, the real environment issue was sidelined and all environmental analysis focused on the effect of the Dabhol Plant with LNG as fuel on the area around the plant and on the sea and on vegetation.

The Sub-Committee feels that even if Dabhol was to have been selected as a site for this project, the negotiating team should not have put certain conditions for counter-balancing the detrimental effects that this project would have had on the environment of the Konkan. The primary occupation of the people of this area is fishing and the villagers of this area have expressed their fears before the Sub-Committee, during its visit to the Project site, that the fish catch is likely to diminish. The Sub-Committee feels that the ultimate test of this being environment-friendly would be that the capacity of the environment to support the people should not be reduced.

If the above had been kept in mind, it should have been made mandatory for the DPC to take such measures as would enhance marine life so that the livelihood of fishermen is not affected. Further conditions should have been imposed to enhance the green cover and preserve the biodiversity of the area.

3.8 How far the project is useful for the development of the State:

There can be no doubt that the availability of reasonably priced, efficient and reliable power supply is an essential concomitant to industrial development. It would not be possible for Maharashtra to retain its premier position as the leading industrial State in the country if there is any shortage of power or if the power supply available in the State is not reliable. Having said this, however, it must be noted that there is a point at which the cost of power becomes a factor that must be considered along with availability and reliability. It is clear, from the discussion in the forgoing chapters, that this is the case in respect of the power from DPC.

We have already pointed out that because of the indeterminate nature of the price of gas, the cost of power per unit will vary widely. This situation will be aggravated because the capacity charge as will as the fuel charge have been denominated in U.S. dollars. As a result, more than 98 percent of the costs of power from this project will be subject to fluctuations on the international currency market. The extent to which estimates of the cost of power will vary on this account is difficult to estimate. It is clear, however, that the cost of such power will be far more than the State can afford to pay. The Sub-Committee is convinced that there are other and better alternatives that have not been critically examined.

There is yet another dimension to the high cost of Enron power that must be carefully considered. Since MSEB has underwritten capacity to the extent of 90 percent, it means that they are under obligation to consume this power at all times. At night, therefore, when demand falls, MSEB will be forced to back down its less costly power in order to consume the high cost of power of DPC. The effect of this on the working of the Board can readily be imagined. The problem seems to be that MSEB has failed to distinguish between its peak-load requirements and its base-load requirements and plan accordingly. The result is that high-cost power will be given precedence over low cost power in the grid, and this is clearly not in the best interest of the State.

CHAPTER IV

FINDINGS AND RECOMMENDATIONS

On the basis of the above recital of facts and circumstances and on the evidence that has surfaced at the time of the Review, the Sub-Committee's findings and recommendations are as under:

1. On the question of competitive bids:

The previous Government has committed a grave impropriety by resorting to private negotiations on a one on one basis with Enron and under circumstances which made the Enron/MSEB arrangement on Dabhol to lack transparency. Although there was no policy formulated for competitive bidding in power projects this has been accepted practice, in the larger public interest, to involve more than one contender. There was no compelling reason not to involve a second contender for Dabhol. Actually, such a thought does not seem to have occurred to anyone at all. Therefore the Sub-Committee strongly disapproves of the one to one negotiations with Enron and is clearly of the view that it violates standard and well-tested norms of propriety for public organisations.

2. On whether there was any secret or off the record negotiations:

Considering the records available with the State Government and the MSEB, we are led to the irresistible conclusion that they are not the only guide to what actually happened. It is reasonably clear that several unseen factors and forces seem to have worked to get Enron what it wanted.

3. On whether the capital cost of the Project is reasonable:

On the basis of the material accessed by the Sub-Committee, it concludes that the capital cost of the DPC project was inflated.

4. On whether undue favours and concessions have been given for the Project:

Several unusual features of the negotiations and final agreement have been pointed out by the Sub Committee in the report which makes it clear that whatever Enron wanted was granted without demur.

5. Whether the rate for power from the Dabhol plant is reasonable:

The Sub-Committee is of the view that because of the denomination of tariff for power in U.S. dollars and other reasons, the consumer will have to pay a much higher price for power than is justified. This is clearly not reasonable.

6. On the environmental aspects of the Project:

The Sub-Committee is of the view that the real environmental issue is whether such a huge power project should be located in such an unpolluted part of Maharashtra and whether there is any other part of the State where it could have been located. Also whether a project of lesser size could help the preservation of the environment better was not gone into. It is evident from the environmental assessment that marine life and plants may have to face problems if adequate care is not taken.

7. On whether the Project is useful to the State:

The Sub-Committee is of the view that such high cost power as Enron envisages will, in the immediate future, and in the long run, adversely affect Maharashtra and the rapid industrialization of the State and its competitiveness.

CONCLUSION

The Sub-Committee, having examined the issues and having listed the deficiencies as above, is unanimously of the view that the arrangement in force is not tenable because of the infirmities pointed out above in the terms and conditions of the contract. It, therefore, recommends that Phase II of the Project should be canceled and Phase I should be repudiated.

[signature]
Sudhir Joshi
Minister for Revenue
& Member

[signature]
Gopinath Munde
Deputy Chief Minister
& Chairman

[signature]
Liladhar Dake
Minister for Industries
& Member

Appendix C: Selected Recommendations and Conclusions from the Parliamentary Standing Committee on Energy, May 29, 1995

Selected Recommendations and Conclusions from the Parliamentary Standing Committee on Energy, May 29, 1995

2. Establishment of a transparent bidding procedure and a set of criteria against which bids could be evaluated is essential for selecting appropriate power companies for Power Projects. Sadly, this was not done until recently. Instead of taking advantage of international experience in promoter selection, the Government preferred to go in for the bilateral route on the plea that in view of non-crystallisation methodologies and lack of investors' confidence the negotiated route was the only option. It was only after the matter was taken up by the Committee that the Centre issued guidelines to State Governments on 18.1.1995 making the competitive bidding route mandatory. Hopefully, the change over to the system of competitive bidding would bring transparency to the business of private sector participation and result in competitive tariff proposals.

5. The tariff structure based on "cost-plus" approach is stated to have advantages in the initial phase because of compatibility with CEA procedure for project approval and SEB's own experience with this form of pricing. Surprisingly, the Ministry of Power has argued that there is nothing wrong with the present cost-plus approach. The Committee does not agree with this view. The Committee feels that private investors appear to have a tendency to inflate costs which would finally translate into higher tariff. Besides, the cost-plus approach has given rise to avoidable controversies. The Committee, therefore, recommends that the Government should examine the desirability of adopting a standard practice of specifying a single rate at which private investors are asked to sell power. Incidentally, the adoption of a simple tariff system will also eliminate the need of offering guaranteed PLF linked return on equity.

6. There are four gas-based and three coal-based power projects in the private sector cleared by the CEA so far. Out of the four gas-based projects, the per megawatt (MW) cost in respect of these projects (Jagrupadu, Godavari, and Puguthan) was between Rs. 3.52 crores and Rs. 3.74 crores, while for Dabhol, the cost per MW was Rs. 4.19 crores. Of the three coal-based projects, the cost per MW of Vishakhpatnam project at Rs. 5.82 crores is considerably higher than the Ib Valley at Rs. 4.82 crores and Mangalore project at Rs. 5.08 crores. BHEL in this connection has pointed out that turnkey costs in respect of projects with BHEL equipment could cost only around Rs. 3.6 crores to 4.3 crores per MW after making suitable adjustments for development cost, inflation and interest during construction. The cost per MW of private projects in general and Dabhol and

Vishakhpatnam in particular appear to be much higher than that indicated by BHEL. The Committee feels that the guaranteed rate of return are tempting the investors to inflate their costs to ensure better returns. According to experts, lack of competitive bidding has led to significant padding in the investment costs. The Committee desires that the Government should ensure that cost of private power projects should be so determined as it conforms to the simple tariff structure recommended in the preceding paragraph. Efforts should also be made to dispel doubts with regard to reasonableness of the cost of private power projects.

10. Power Purchase Agreement (PPA) is basically a commercial contractual agreement between the SEB [State Electricity Board] and the generating company. The PPA allocates the risks associated with a power project, including fuel prices and other operating costs, financing costs, construction costs and various performance parameters. The Committee feels that it will be useful if a measure of uniformity could be achieved on the factors common to PPAs. The scrutiny of PPAs should be made a part of techno-economic appraisal by the Central Electricity Authority. The Committee desires that instructions in this regard should be issued early.

11. The confidentiality of Power Purchase Agreement and Fuel Purchase Agreements (FPAs) have sparked intense debate in the media and in various other forums and there is widespread perception of biased contracts. It is observed that a confidentiality clause has been inserted in the PPAs for Dabhol Power Company and some others. Such lack of transparency is regrettable, as it precludes public scrutiny and gives rise to avoidable misgivings. The Committee, therefore, desires that the Government should issue guidelines requiring SEBs/State Governments to make all the PPAs and FPAs public documents with the exception of any confidential data contained therein.

Appendix D: Correspondence Between the Government of India and the World Bank

INTERNATIONAL DEVELOPMENT ASSOCIATION
Washington DC,
USA
Cable :____

April 30, 1993

Mr. M.S. Ahluwalia,
Secretary
Department of Economic Affairs
Ministry of Finance
North Block
New Delhi 110 001
India.

SUBJECT: Proposed Dabhol Power Project

Dear Mr. Ahluwalia·

    As requested in Mr. Khurana's fax to Mr. Bauer dated March 12, 1993, we have examined the proposed Dabhol Power Project of the Enron Power Development Corporation for which we were requested to consider World Bank financing. Our analysis based on the parameters provided to us indicated that the LNG- Based project as presently formulated is not economically viable, and thus could not be financed by the Bank. We have reached the conclusion on the two following grounds :

    a)   the proposed 2015 MW project is too large for base load operation in the Maharashtra State Electricity Board (MSEB) system. Project design is inflexible and would result in uneconomic plant dispatch (lower variable cost coal power would be replaced by much higher cost LNG power) in order to utilize the full amount of LNG to be contracted. This adversely affects the economic viability of the project and would place a heavy financial burden on the MSEB ; and

    b)   the project is not part of the least Cost sequence for Maharashtra power development. Local coal and gas are the preferred choices for base load generation. Even when taking into account the fact that India will face increasing difficulties in meeting the growing demand for its local coal and gas and allowing for the differential costs of emission controls, imported coal-not LNG-would appear to be the next best choice for base load generation for MSEB.

The attached note summarizes the main issues and details our conclusion for your information.
    Given the standing which the companies sponsoring the proposed Dabhol Power Project enjoy in their field of business, it would appear worthwhile for you to explore possible ways to sustain their interest in investing in India's energy sector, in particular to see whether it would be economically feasible to reshape the project to serve higher value intermediate load in the Western Region.

    I would like to take this opportunity to assure you once again that the bank strongly supports your government's private power initiatives and is keen to consider other private power project proposals, including a reshaped Dabhol project, which you may wish to submit to us for Bank financing.

Sincerely yours,

Sd/-
Heinz Vergin
Director
India Country Department.

3

**INDIA
DABHOL POWER PROJECT**

Introduction

1.   In July 1992, ENRON power Development Corporation, (ENRON, USA) and the Maharashtra State Electricity Board (MSEB) entered into a Memorandum of Understanding for Enron to set up a 2550 MW power Station to build, own and operate basis, at Dabhol, about 150 miles South of Bombay in the state of Maharashtra. This proposal was subsequently scaled down to 2015 MW and is referred to in this note as the project. The project would run in base load on natural gas, imported from Qatar in the form of Liquefied Natural Gas (LNG). The size of the project in base-load operation, matches output of one LNG production train. A two stage development is envisaged stage 1 involves construction of 690 MW, stage 2 an expansion to about 2015 MW, consisting of 3 X 635 MW combined cycle units and 110 MW additional gas turbine peaking capacity. Stage I is scheduled to be commissioned in the first quarter of 1996 (assuming financing is arranged by the end of 1993), running initially on distillate fuel oil. Stage 2 is scheduled to be commissioned in 1998, if the financing and the contract for the supply of LNG can be finalized by the end of 1993.

Power Purchase Agreement (PPA)

2   The power purchase agreement (PPA) provides for separate capacity and energy charges. MSEB would pay not only the capacity charge but also the energy charge if the generation (due to MSEB's despatch) does not reach the agreed minimum level (currently envisaged by ENRON to be 80-85%). ENRON has indicated that it is prepared to guarantee a 90% availability and its calculations assume dispatch at 90% plant load factor. Since the plant is designed to consume the output of one LNG train and in light of the PPA provisions, MSEB will have no option but to run the plant in base load with minimal variation.

Power Market

3.   The addition of a 2015 MW station, in forced base-load operation, would place a significant constraint in MSEB's power system. System simulations show that while the project would provide additional generation to help most increasing loads in peak periods, it would displace lower cost coal-fired generation in the off-peak periods.

4.   The Western Region system and India as a whole have surplus generation capacity in off-peak periods (8-10 hours during night time. Although the output of coal-fired stations is reduced during the off-peak periods within occupational constraints, system frequencies commonly exceed 50 Hz off peak, a concrete sign of surplus capacity. The imbalance between base load generation (mainly coal) and peak-to-intermediate load generation (mainly hydro supplemented by natural gas in combined cycle generation) has worsened steadily during the 1980s and is likely to worsen further in the 1990s and possible even beyond. Surplus coal-based power in the off-peak periods is likely to continue in the foreseeable future.

5.   Since MSEB's system cannot fully absorb the output of the project in off-peak periods, MSEB have to sell surplus LNG based power to other states. At best, MSEB may be able to sell coal-based power in the Southern Region, at or close to its variable generating cost, in off-peak periods. As a result it would incur financial losses. LNG generation at a variable cost of about paise 150/kwh would displace coal-based power costing paise 30/kwh. This loss, adjusted to economic terms, would have to be included in the economic analysis as a project cost and thus reduce project benefits.

Market for LNG Power in India

6.   Natural gas-fired combined cycle stations provide an attractive option for intermediate to base load generation. In the Indian system, given the current and the projected availability of lower cost coal fired base load generation during off-peak periods, combined cycle stations are economically attractive mainly in intermediate load service. The availability of natural gas constraints currently the use of gas for power generation. Imported LNG has a potential market niche supplementing domestic natural

gas. Targeting the Dabhol Project to take advantage of this niche would require modifications in the project design and size as well as in the PPA. Given the relative high cost of LNG compared to local natural gas, a comparison between LNG based power and coal based power in intermediate load generation would still be necessary to ensure that this indeed meets the least-cost condition. Due to its higher capital cost, a coal fueled station is generally not competitive in intermediate load service, but the high cost of LNG increases coal's competitiveness.

Macro-economic considerations

7. The implementation of the project would place a significant long-term claim on India's foreign exchange resources. The estimated annual fuel cost is about US $ 500 million, subject to escalation as provided for in the PPA (a fuel cost pass through to MSEB is envisaged). Contractually, capacity payments in foreign currency would start at about US $ 175 million (70% of India's merchandise imports, only considered here) in 1996 and escalating at 5% per annum, reaching US $ 400 million in 2015.

8. Bank projections indicate that (a) the current account and external reserve positions, and the external debt/expert ratio would improve (b) the debt service ratio would rise initially, but fall to 22% in FY 1998 (compared to 26% in FY 93) and (c) foreign reserves in FY 98 would be at over 10 $ billion or less annual foreign exchange claims are considered affordable by India in this scenario. For example, in year 2000, fuel import for the project would account for about 1.2% of India's merchandise imports, capital service would account for about 1.7 % of India's merchandise exports. There is down side risk of much lower than the projected 5.6% annual GDP growth; and a much less favorable balance of payments and reserve position could emerge.

9. Most critical for the project with a non-tradable output (and with no direct foreign exchange earnings) is the relative growth of India's exports and imports. Bank projections show export growth consistently exceeding the growth of imports, contributing to the relative base case set of indicators outlined above. Import demand depends on the pace of further liberalization, and on the performance of the energy sector, in particular the domestic production of oil and gas. Price of oil is an important variable; a Bank sensitivity analysis shows that a 33% increase could lead into foreign reserves declining to half the projected reserve. While such risks reinforce the need for prudent macro-economic policies and vigorous export promotion, the project would even in that scenario still be considered affordable for India.(1)

10. Assuming that the alternative would be to build additional coal-fired stations using local coal, the outflow would be limited to debt service for foreign borrowing, foreign exchange. Such foreign exchange outflow would be significantly below those of ENRON project (about 30-40% only of the Enron outflow) and would be even lower depending on the extent of domestic manufacturers' participation in the equipment supply. The foreign exchange outflow resulting from the development of coal-fired generation using imported coal would be much closer to the outflows of the ENRON project (the difference would depend on the source of equipment and the possibly different escalation of LNG and coal prices).

11. It has been argued that in the absence of the project, India would not implement the domestic or the imported coal option, due to financing constraints. True additionally of the project is limited to the foreign equity, even as concerns that component, Enron's partners (GE and Bechtel) might well invest in coal based power projects in India in case the project does not proceed. ENRON is unlikely to participate in coal projects, but may be interested by another gas-based project. The major part of the project financing proposed to be provided by the Bank, US Exim Bank and domestic capital market, should be available to finance reasonable alternative projects, such as a series of 500 MW coal projects using imported coal. Not proceeding with the project may somewhat delay power development, but it is unlikely to cause a lasting setback to India's private power program.

---

1. India should according to the considerations, afford to commit to number of power projects of this size or smaller private power projects in the 1990s. The main question then becomes which projects it should pursue and whether LNG base-load power is among the high priority options.

5

Cost and value of LNG Power

12. ENRON indicated that the total cost of power, in base load generation at 90% plant load, is about US cents 7.0/kwh, of which about US cents 3.3/kwh is for capacity. Assuming industrial sales in areas close to the project location and on additional investment of 20% for transmission and distribution and assuming 10% for system losses, the average cost at the consumer level would at the minimum be US cents 7.4/kwh. This corresponds to about Rs. 2.4/kwh in 1993 prices. These figures do not include import duties and taxes on equipment and LNG. The former has been reduced to 20% in India's FY 94 budget, the later is understood to be at 16%. Using these figures, the resulting retail revenue from LNG power would have to be Rs. 2.4/kwh in 1993 prices, equivalent to Rs. 4.6/kwh in 1998 prices, with no provision for administrative and other MSEB overheads (or cross-subsidization of agricultural and residential consumers, para. 14).

13. The cost of LNG based power is comparable to that of diesel generation and lower than that of diesel pumping. The willingness to pay for electricity by industrial consumers has been estimated at about Rs. 2.2/kwh in the Western region and Rs. 2.4/kwh in Bombay in the second Maharashtra appraisal report, below the cost of LNG power. The Bank's standard project economic analysis concludes that the project is not viable. The project therefore would have to be justified as a special effort to meet the electricity demands of consumers expressing a willingness to pay higher tariffs for guaranteed and/or additional supply at system peak periods. However, it remains to be established that a demand for such power exists.

14. Electricity prices given in 1998 prices above demonstrate the need for substantial tariff adjustments for MSEB. Its current average revenue is about Rs. 1.4/kwh, the revenue from the most lucrative industrial consumers is in the Rs. 2-2.5/kwh range. Prices for industrial consumers would at the minimum have to be doubled in nominal terms to recover the cost of LNG power. This indicates annual increases of about 15-20% against the Bank's 5-6% inflation estimates. It should be noted that to the extent that the industrial customers actually take LNG power. However, the above tariff would not provide for cross-subsidization hence an across the board adjustment instead of a special LNG power tariff for specified consumers would be needed.

Load Forecasts

15. System simulations referred to in the above discussion use CEA load projection for Maharashtra. The projections assume an annual load growth of over 7% in the 1990s and about 6% in the following decade. This projection is higher than the forecast used in the appraisal in the 2nd Maharashtra Power Project. The later was based on Maharashtra's estimated capacity in supply, which due to financial constraints was judged insufficient to meet CEA's forecast.

16. MSEB maintains that CEA's projections is too low, on the basis of pending applications from industries for additional supply not considered in the CEA projection. Such application amount to about 4100 MW. MSEB's assessment is that about 50% of these applications would materialize, thus increasing the peak load by 2100 MW by 1997 at a 77 % load factor. This would absorb all LNG power and eliminate the projected surpluses. Should this load scenario materialize, surpluses would indeed diminish. However, this would not invalidate the conclusion that on LNG based power plant operating in base load is not the least cost option for expanding power supply.

17. The suggested load increase is unproven and the proposed high forecast is not a suitable basis for evaluating the project. Three points warrant attention regarding the proposed high forecast. First, the full additionality of the loads in pending applications is questionable and the resulting growth rate for industrial electricity consumption is unproven. MSEB's industrial sales in FY 93 were about 16400 Gwh and are projected to increase to about 22300 Gwh in the CEA forecast, adding about 6000 Gwh MSEB's proposed additional load to be connected by that year corresponds to 12000 Gwh. Under this assumption industrial load would double, i.e. grow at an average rate of about 20% for 4 years, compared to CEA's already respectable 8% average annual growth.

---

2. Given the large size of the project to MSEB system, time allocation of the output to the most lucrative consumers of course somewhat questionable. The locational advantage is clear the project will generate power not far from the main load centre in Maharashtra.

6

Second, the willingness of the applicants on MSEB's 4100 MW list to pay the above mentioned price, involving more than doubling the current industrial tariffs, has not been tested. Applications may well reflect expectations of the relative low electricity prices continuing. Before a high forecast could be adopted as the basis of the analysis of the new state-wide forecast (involving the review of CEA forecasts and pending applications) would need to be undertaken, taking price explicitly into account in the forecast. Third, MSEB is unable to connect the new load gradually between 1993 and 1997 as it does not have additional generation capacity, The load is unlikely to wait until 1996-1998 and then come in over 1-2 year period; a more gradual increase is likely.

Conclusions :

18   Although the ongoing review of the methodology would require marginal adjustments in some of the assumptions, it is highly unlikely that they would change the results
of the analysis. The main conclusions of the analysis are summarized below :

(a) The project is not a least-cost choice for base load power generation compared to Indian coal and local gas. Even if domestic fuels are not available, imported coal would be the least-cost option for base-load generation for MSEB with current environmental standards. The additional requirement of fuel-gas desulphurization would narrow coal's advantage, but in all likelihood not eliminate it; an environmental premium would be required to close the gap. In addition to lower fuel cost, the coal alternative is more attractive due to its flexibility, capacity can be added in 500 MW units in steps to meet the growing demand instead of a 2,000 MW in 1998 in the project;

(b) The unique features and risks of this LNG-based project (large minimum consumption, dependence on one power generator and on one LNG supplier) need to be considered; they offset LNG's environmental benefits over coal. The LNG price escalation cost is still to be confirmed for the project; international practice is to be the price of LNG to oil or coal price;

(c) ENRON's current proposal would require MSEB to dispatch the plant as a base load unit at 80-85% minimum plant factor(referred to as plant load factor, PLF, in India). This would prevent the operational flexibility of a combined cycle plant,

(d) Stipulations of MSEB power operations indicate that the project would add more capacity than needed to meet the projected load growth in 1998 and would also result in uneconomic plant dispatch (lower variable cost coal power would be replaced by much higher variable cost LNG power). This would adversely affect the economic viability of the project and place a heavy financial burden on the MSEB; and

(e) Substantial adjustment in electricity tariffs would be required to recover cost of the project from the consumers and to safeguard MSEB's financial position. Given the large share of the project in MSEB's power supply in the initial years, across-the-board adjustment would be required. Adjustments limited to special industrial consumer categories would not be sufficient as their capability to continue to cross-subsidize, by paying more than the already high cost of LNG power, would be limited.

April 30,1993.

ANNEXURE 9

LETTER DATED 26/7/93 FROM THE WORLD BANK TO THE GOI

The World Bank
INTERNATIONAL BANK FOR RECONSTRUCTION AND DEVELOPMENT
INTERNATIONAL DEVELOPMENT ASSOCIATION

1815 N. Street, NW
Washington, DC
USA

July 26, 1993

Mr. R. Vasudevan
Secretary Ministry of Power
Shram Shakti Bhavan
Rafi Marg, New Delhi 110 001
INDIA

Dear Mr. Vasudevan :

Subject: Proposed Dabhol Power Project

1. This responds to your letter of June 18th which acknowledged my letter of April 30 in which we had, on the request of the DEA, provided a first evaluation of the Dabhol Power Project with a view to its suitability for possible Bank-financing. With reference to that evaluation you had suggested that we revisit with the concerned GOI authorities several key parameters employed in our project analysis. A series of meeting with these authorities were held in early July and our conclusions are summarized below.

2. Regarding the load forecast for the Maharashtra market, the recent protracted discussions have led to reconfirm CEA's 14th Electric Power Survey (EPS) as the most realistic forecast on which to base our analysis. As regards the important assumptions about the future performance of MSEB's existing system, we propose to reflect in our analysis the understandings reached during the processing of the 2nd Maharashtra Power Project in 1992 together with additional information obtained from and received with MSEB subsequently. However, we cannot accept the more pessimistic scenario recently provided by MSEB according to which the existing system is projected to decline in efficiency. If this were to be indeed the current best projection, determined action should be taken with priority to reverse this projected deterioration rather than accepting it as a given fact in the analysis of new investments.

3. As regards our assumptions about MSEB's investment program, we propose to go with the information received from MSEB upto June. We are not in a position to verify or comment on the delays in ongoing and planned projects which have been reported more recently; however, we are finding it difficult to accord added justification to the Dabhol project based on the most recently discovered slippage's in MSEB's ongoing and planned least-cost program.

4. After extensive further review of the above parameters and detailed review of the analytical framework and costing assumptions we reconfirm our earlier conclusion that the Dabhol project as presently formulated is not economically justified and thus could not be financed by the Bank.

5. In our assessment, the project is too large to enter the MSEB system in 1998. The proposed base-load operation would result in uneconomic plant dispatch, as already existing lower variable cost coal power would be replaced by higher cost LNG power. At the same time, the potentially significant contribution to improving the operation of MSEB's power system that a major combined cycle power station could make would be substantially undermined by forcing this capacity into base load operation.

6. As a logical step, it would be now desirable to examine possibilities to strengthen the economic and financial viability of the project by reshaping the project to primarily serve higher-value intermediate load and to realize the benefits of improved system operations attributable to the addition of the combined cycle

capacity. This would require consideration of a large consumer base, e.g. the Western Region, to share the risks and cost of the project; and possible adjustments in the proposed phasing and timing of the project. Such reshaping may strengthen the economic justification of the project so as to warrant Bank support. Please note that all these suggestions assume that as presented by ENRON, the full output of one LNG train needs to be consumed in India and cannot be shared with other customers so as to enable project sponsors and MSEB to proceed in Maharashtra with a smaller project better suited to MSEB's needs alone.

7. Given the standing which the companies sponsoring the proposed Dabhol project enjoy in their field of business, we continue to consider it worthwhile for your Government to pursue the benefits of LNG based generation by a reformulated Dhabol project could bring to the overall efficiency of a growing system in the Western Region of India. In such a reformulation, care also needs to be taken to sustain the interest of the sponsors in investing in India's energy sector. In that context we have recently been approached by the sponsors who used the meeting to underscore two main points: the seriousness of their proposal with regard to their advanced status of their efforts to secure a timely supply of LNG and the need to come to closure with Government on the Power Purchase Agreement(PPA). In response to our observation that the Government will find it difficult to sign the PPA when the Bank analysis points out that only a modified project might pass the feasibility test for possible Bank financing, the sponsors informed us that the PPA envisages the implementation of the project in two distinct phases and provides considerable flexibility with regard to the start and modalities of Phase II provided that the LNG up-take in due course equals at least one train of LNG.

8. I am conveying the substance of our recent discussion with the sponsors in order to suggest that your Government may want to carefully examine the flexibility provided by the PPA in order to ascertain what risks it would take if it were to come to closure with the sponsors on the PPA which, while committing the sponsors to your power development, would at the same time provide the flexibility to reshape the timing and modalities of Phase II along the lines described in paragraph 6 above.

9. While these risks would have to be weighed by your Government, we could assist, if it were to be agreeable to you, in further exploring the possibilities to reshape the Dabhol project in direct technical discussion with the project sponsors. To ensure that your office and MSEB are kept abreast of these direct technical discussions, we could minute their substance for your information. I would appreciate your advice on the start of such direct discussions with the sponsors or any other way in which we could be helpful to move the project toward economic and financial feasibility.

10. In conclusion, I would like to assure you again that the Bank strongly supports your Government initiative to enlist the participation of private investors in India's power development and stands ready to be of assistance in translating proposals into tangible investments.

With best regards,

Sincerely yours,

Sd/-
Heinz Vergin
Director
India Country Department

cc: Messrs M.S .Ahluwalia, N.K. Singh
U.K.Mukhopadhyay, A.M.Nimbalkar